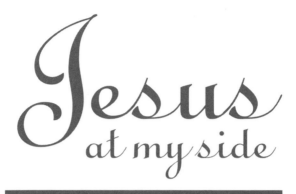

Jesus
at my side

365 Reflections on His Words

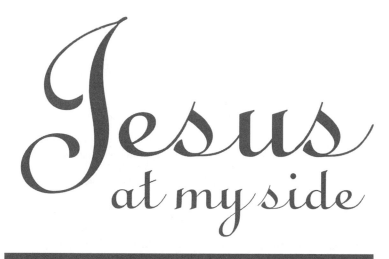

Jesus
at my side

365 Reflections on His Words

Julie Dortch Cragon

Our Sunday Visitor Publishing Division
Our Sunday Visitor, Inc.
Huntington, IN 46750

Nihil Obstat:
Msgr. Michael Heintz, Ph.D.
Censor Librorum

Imprimatur:
✠ Kevin C. Rhoades
Bishop of Fort Wayne-South Bend
May 3, 2012

ISBN: 978-1-59276-943-8 (Inventory No. T1152)
eISBN: 978-1-61278-223-2
LCCN: 2012934468

Interior design by Desiree Korhorn
Cover design by Lindsey Riesen
Cover art by Rose Walton, rosewaltonart@aol.com

PRINTED IN THE UNITED STATES OF AMERICA

Contents

Introduction

Each of these 365 days of meditation includes the words of Jesus, a short meditation, and a prayer challenge for today to put His words into action. What do Jesus' words mean to us today? How can we use His words to build up one another? Where can we make a difference?

As manager and part-owner of St. Mary's Bookstore in Nashville, Tennessee, I have the privilege of working with people and serving people every day who inspire, who proclaim, who teach, and who witness to the words of Jesus.

Jesus' words are for us. We are challenged to read His words daily and to listen to them in the context of our own lives, in our ordinary experiences. This is not an interpretation of the Gospels but a meditation on what Jesus is saying to us today. Each day, we may fit our own experiences into His words. Each year, we may find something different in His words. Each time we hear His words, something will challenge us on our journey. Jesus' words are truth, and in His words we find peace and guidance and, most of all, love.

"Why were you looking for me? Did you not know that I must be in my Father's house?"

LUKE 2:49

Each New Year brings new lists. Whether in my mind or on paper, I look for ways to improve physically or spiritually, to better myself or my business or my home, or to improve relationships or my surroundings. If I fail miserably, I just start fresh the next day. After all, I have the entire year and it's not about stressing over the tasks. It's about what brings joy.

Jesus asks in His first words to us on this first day of a New Year, why are we looking? If we want joy; if we want our day, our week, our year to improve, we must spend time in our Father's house. Stop searching. Stop looking. Just go. Whether we are physically standing in our Father's house or spending time with Him alone in prayer and meditation, Jesus wants to be first in our lives. He wants us to include Him in our family lives, our daily routines, our businesses, our play, our days, and our nights. He wants us to talk to Him, to rely on Him, to visit Him, and in return He wants to share His life with us. Jesus challenges us on this first day of a New Year to stop all the looking. We know where He is; where He must be. Spend time with Him.

"Allow it now, for thus it is fitting for us to fulfill all righteousness."

MATTHEW 3:15

I love things stark white. Clean. Neat. Now don't get me wrong. My house is rarely clean and neat unless I have had help. Nor is my desk or my car or anything else. But I do like the idea. I read magazines and labels and watch shows about how to keep our worldly goods fresh. When we were first married, my husband and I bought a beautiful white couch. However, each child who graced our presence came with their own set of possible stains. I scrubbed and used Clorox and spot-treated to keep that couch white and looking new. But life is just messy, especially with multiple people involved.

Jesus says we must allow the cleansing. Just do it. Do it so all will be right. As John baptizes Jesus, the Fathers' voice from above announces that He is pleased with His Son. The Father is pleased when we begin with Baptism. We are nourished by the waters. Cleansed. Every time we renew our baptismal promises, every time we maintain our beliefs, the Father is pleased and all is right. Sure we all have our own set of possible stains, but every day is a new day and a new possibility to renew our life in Christ, to be made stark white. Take it. It is fitting.

"It is written: / 'One does not live by bread alone, / but by every word that comes forth from the mouth of God.'"

MATTHEW 4:4

The fresh smell of breads and pastries as we enter one of the multiple bread companies that have cropped up in every city may make us think that we could live by bread alone. There would be no problem in variety; all shapes, sizes, and flavors available, sliced or whole loaf. My son and I stopped for soup bowls at Bread and Company one day when he had a half day of school. As I looked around I noticed people gathered, not just for the bread, but for the company. Moms and dads with their children, business men and women, college kids with computers, and many others gathered for good conversation as well as bread.

Jesus has fasted for 40 days and 40 nights and He is hungry. But He will not be tempted to follow the commands of the evil one. He is nourished by the words of God alone. God alone will He follow and God alone will He obey even though He is very hungry and it would be very simple. It is not time. He waits and, as we know, He multiplies the loaves and He breaks the bread and He nourishes in the company of others. As we gather, as the time is made right, we are nourished by the Word. As well as the bread.

"It is written: / 'You shall worship the Lord, your God, / and him alone shall you serve.'"

LUKE 4:8

There is just something about serving others that makes us feel good about ourselves. It's in our make-up. We serve our families, our friends, our parents, our communities, and our church. Sometimes we do so much for others that we wonder when we'll get our turn. We serve so many in so many different ways that we can get tired. Oh sure, we still get the job done, but sometimes the more we do, the more we are expected to do. I know when I am worn down. I often can lose it at the tiniest request. "Hey Mom, can you wash my jeans?" "Can you drive me to Target?" "Can you pick up milk?" "Can you gift wrap?" "Can you come down? A customer has a question?" Can you? Can you? Can you?

Jesus speaks directly to us. Worship God and serve only Him so our attitude of serving changes. We serve with the idea in mind that every act is serving God and therefore the joy to serve will never cease. Give to God. Pray to God. Love God, and all the work we do in serving others will serve God. Let's keep our priorities straight. Serve God and in serving Him, we will serve others with joy. I can. I can. I can.

January 5

"It also says, 'You shall not put the Lord, your God, to the test.'"

We can often feel tested by our children, our neighbors, our coworkers, our employees, our customers, or our boss. We know what it's like to be put out on a limb and told to save ourselves. We are dangling out there, and we know we can do it, but we must wonder why we got pushed out there in the beginning. My children have pushed the "time for bed" issue until I finally get angry and the next day asked me to help them because they are too tired. I have had neighbors who constantly complained and then asked to borrow our tools. I have had an employee who continually tested my patience for no reason as if she wanted to see if I am a good enough Christian to overlook her shortcomings and hold on to her no matter what occurred. Frustrated me to no end! Who likes to be tested to prove themselves? Can't we all just believe in one another enough not to push?

Jesus says the same thing. Don't test me. Don't push. You know I love you and you know that no matter how far you stray, I will come for you. But wouldn't our relationship be a lot easier if we just did not go there in the first place? Jesus reminds us that He will always love us, always take us back, and always forgive us uncondi-

10

tionally. He is the One who will overlook our shortcomings. He is our all. Trust Him.

"What are you looking for?"

JOHN 1:38

We are a helpful bunch. Seems we are constantly asking others if they need help. Day after day we ask our coworkers, our customers, our neighbors, "Can I help you find something?" I know I ask my kids if they need help as they are rummaging through their dresser drawers or through the laundry looking for a specific shirt. I ask my employees if they need help finding boxes for merchandise or a category for a book to be shelved. As we know, they can say "no" out of preoccupation or they can stop and give the specifics that help us to speed along the search.

The same goes with Jesus. He asks us what we are looking for. We come to Him. We sit with Him in silence or we take time out of our busy day and He wants to know. What are we looking for? This is our chance. Our opportunity. We have chosen to take time with Him and He gives us the chance to tell Him what we want from Him. We can continue to search through life preoccupied with our surroundings or we can stop and fill Him in on the specifics. Tell Him.

"Come, and you will see."

JOHN 1:39

Why does it seem that everyone questions our call to come and see? Constantly suspicious, our children, our coworkers, and our neighbors all want to know why. "What ya need?" "Why?" "Do I have to?" "What is it?" Don't we just want to scream, "Just come and you'll see." or "Just forget it!" Just come because we asked you to come and see. We want you to see.

We are constantly beckoned by Jesus and today is no different. Listen to His voice. He says, "Come." Come to Him and you will see that He is the Way. He is the Truth. He is the Light. He will lead us and guide us and together we will make a difference in a world that oftentimes seems filled with difficulties. In this particular passage the Apostle has asked Him where He is staying and on this particular day we know that He is staying with us. He is staying in our days and in our nights. He is staying in our good times and in our bad times. He is staying in our hearts. Come, and you will see.

"It is I. Do not be afraid."

JOHN 6:20

$\mathcal{I}$ do not like scary movies. When ads come on the television for an upcoming horror film and are shown between children's shows or sports shows, I get angry. What has happened to the good ole family channels? Even when they hide their eyes, my children can still catch a glimpse of some awful happening. Sometimes they jump when I walk up to kiss them goodnight. They say, "Who's there?" when I walk through the hallway. I have to constantly say, "It's just me. Do not be afraid."

Jesus speaks to us and we should listen to His words in a more general way. Yes, He is telling us not to fear because He is in our midst. He tells us not to be scared, but He also says for us to go out and take His message and to not be afraid of what other people think or say. He tells us that with Him in our midst, we have nothing to fear. Stop worrying about the darkness. Stop hiding. Go out and do the will of the Father and share our faith because it is Jesus who walks beside us. It is He in our midst and there is nothing to fear. Be not afraid.

"The Spirit of the Lord is upon me, / because he has anointed me / to bring glad tidings to the poor. / He has sent me to proclaim liberty to captives / and recovery of sight to the blind, / to let the oppressed go free, / and to proclaim a year acceptable to the Lord."

LUKE 4:18, 19

$\mathcal{A}$ year acceptable to the Lord! As we walk around or watch television, we can easily see how unacceptable our world is today. In our communities, we see children who cannot play together and neighbors who squabble over property lines and adults talking bad about one another, slandering names. In our cities we see violence and poverty and stealing and cheating. In our countries we see war and death and destruction. Unacceptable. Prayer is the answer. Prayer changes things. Mary has delivered the message more than once to pray the Rosary for peace; for our neighborhoods, for our cities, for our countries.

Jesus tells us that He has come to clear up all these problems. He is right here in our midst day in and day out and He was sent to free the world of their own misery. To bring glad tidings. To liberate. To recover. To free. We must believe in Jesus' power to save our neighborhoods and our cities and our countries. He is sent to free us from our blindness and to open our eyes to the gifts He offers. Through Him, we can make a change. Listen to His words. Help make this a year acceptable to the Lord. Pray.

January 10

"Woman, how does your concern affect me? My hour has not yet come."
JOHN 2:4

*D*oesn't it drive you crazy when something "comes up" and you know just the right person to go to for help, and when you explain everything and await their jump on the bandwagon, they respond, "And?" As in, "What does that have to do with me?" We like everyone to work together. We are team builders. Whether at work or in our families or in our communities, we like everyone to join in and help out. But timing is everything. Sometimes others can't help because they already have commitments and then again some try to help regardless of their commitments because family and friends mean everything.

Jesus shows His constant care and concern for our needs. Often, our timing is what throws off our requests and God's answer seems to be "Not yet." Despite the improper timing of Mary's need for her Son's power, He cared so deeply for her concern for the groom and for the situation that He did as she asked. She never doubted. Mary trusted completely that her Son would do as she asked. Even though He asked what it had to do with Him, she knew in her heart that He would come through for her and He did. In God's time, He will jump on the bandwagon and He will fill our true needs. Never doubt.

"Fill the jars with water.... Draw some out now and take it to the headwaiter."

JOHN 2:7, 8

I am standing before about one hundred peers, not quite sure what I'm going to say. I have long since thrown away my notes I've worked on for a week, deciding just to accept the recognition, thank the group, and move on. I have prayed for mornings and waited for something to say but nothing comes. My mother approaches the podium before me and leads right in to me having something to say for both of us by telling a great story of how an old street guy she met before Mass that morning told her what to say and how to speak from her heart. Then, her heart steps back and it's my heart's turn. Only my mother could turn an old street guy's advice into such eloquence. As I spoke, the words poured out of the importance of family and friends, past and present, in life and in business, and I have no idea what I said. There was laughter and nodding of heads and smiles and finally applause, and I was done. He made me look great and all I could do was be grateful.

Jesus does not just get us to fill the jars and deliver the goods. He does not just take care of the situation, but He makes those who have provided the wine look great in the process. Jesus reminds us that we have to put forth some effort. Fill the jars. Pray. Draw the water. Deliver. And through it all, He is in our midst. Trust in Him. Jesus will come through for us and in the process He will make us look really good. Just wait.

January 12

"Take these out of here, and stop making my Father's house a marketplace."

JOHN 2:16

*M*arketplaces can be incredibly hectic. Buying and selling and talking and haggling over prices. I am fortunate in our church goods business that prices are pretty much set by our vendors with little room for haggling. But where I can relate to the huge disruption in our Father's house are the distractions for me over the "things" from my "marketplace" that I find in the church. The distraction of the candles being crooked or the altar boy's Velcro on his alb not being put together evenly. Concelebrating priests not wearing matching vestments or at least close to matching. I oftentimes have to remember that it's just not about the candles and the clothing and the hardware. The person we are there for is not the one who walks down the aisle and delivers the homily but the one who is present in the tabernacle, at the consecration.

Jesus speaks to us firmly today about His Father's house. He leaves no room for exceptions. Take out whatever it is that causes the distraction in our minds and our hearts and our physical selves. Today we are called to envision what our Church would be like if there was endless talking and constant confusion. There has to be one place in this hectic world, in our busy lives, where we can go and pray in peace and quiet. The Father's house is to be a place that is respected, and we are called to be an example of the importance of that respect. Be fully present.

January 13

"Destroy this temple and in three days I will raise it up."

John 2:19

I think that most of us have had times when we question God's words or actions. For me, it has regularly circled around my children or my business, such as, why a child hasn't gotten in to a certain high school or college or an employee has left for another job. Temporary confusion for my life that seems not to make sense. And yet later I see clearly that He has had a plan. He has provided a better fit for my child in school, a better fit for my former employee in a new job, and a great fit for a new employee.

Jesus tells us to stay in tune to His words and the path He leads us on will eventually make sense. We must remain as children on a walk of faith. We must trust the one who leads us. It is our responsibility to study and to understand so that someday all things will come together and mesh in our lives. "Destroy this temple" — sure? "Raise it in three days" — okay — what's He talking about? If we take this passage literally, it's hard to understand, but in the Resurrection, everything is seen clearly. He is crucified. He is raised. The message to us is in the rest of the story. As many times in our lives, the immediate message is difficult to understand. But if we hang on, trust, walk in faith, we see He has a plan for us. In the Resurrection.

"The wind blows where it wills and you can hear the sound it makes, but you do not know where it comes from or where it goes; so it is with everyone who is born of the Spirit."

JOHN 3:8

I have sat in the audience of many powerful speakers and thought as they finish, "Wow! What a powerhouse! They hit me right where I am today." Sometimes the message may sink in later and I feel compelled to pop myself in the forehead. Tornados. Whirlwinds. Powerful Christian speakers. If we have never experienced one in person, we have seen the effect on TV or read about them. They pass through, and we may only hear a strange noise or a quiet message. We may not see their paths, but we see the results of their passage and are left with a deep impression. It was that way for me at a women's conference when Johnnette Benkovic spoke, at a men's conference when Fr. Larry Richards spoke, and at a book conference when Fr. James Martin spoke.

Jesus tells us that we who believe can feel the result of the Spirit being a part of our lives. We may not physically feel the Spirit, but we know He lives within us and guides us. There is no magic, no smoke, and no mirrors. The wonder is simply the Spirit and the path He takes remains deep. Need He say more?

"Amen, amen, I say to you, we speak of what we know and we testify to what we have seen, but you people do not accept our testimony. If I tell you about earthly things and you do not believe, how will you believe if I tell you about heavenly things?"

JOHN 3:11, 12

I remember my mom used to say, "I can talk until I'm blue in the face, and you kids just won't listen." My mom taught us all the simple things in life that could have saved us a lot of grief. Look both ways before crossing the street. Brush your teeth. Stay in school. Be kind to your teachers. She didn't always explain that we could get hit by a car or pay thousands in dental bills later in life or maintain a better job or someday have our teachers as clients or customers. She expected us to believe her because she was mom and she knew best. Then there were the harder, less tangible lessons about God and faith and hope and love. I guess if it took until we were getting our teeth drilled to learn the simple lessons she taught, maybe she was actually walking around "blue in the face" most days trying to teach us the things we could not touch and see.

Jesus tells us to listen to Him. His words are of the utmost importance. Like news from a friend that we strain to hear in a whisper, we must hang on Jesus' every word. He knows what we're going through. He has been there. He has seen it all. And there is a much better ending if we just follow Him in the simple teachings. If we think we've seen it all with our blue-faced mom, Jesus says, we won't even believe what's in store in Heaven for those who trust in Him. Accept His testimony. Listen.

January 16

For God so loved the world that he gave his only Son, so that everyone who believes in him might not perish but might have eternal life. For God did not send his Son into the world to condemn the world, but that the world might be saved through him.

JOHN 3:16, 17

In our world today, it seems that everything has to be over the top. Our outfits are so cute, our hair is so long, we are so in need of a manicure, our children are so bored, we are so busy, and so on and so on. Nothing is simple anymore. My daughter uses the phrase "I so need that." Now I hate to so disappoint her, but I happen to know that she doesn't need anything much less "so need" something. So, why are we always putting so much emphasis on so many things? Perhaps we have turned into a world of "so much more." We consider our needs, our wants, our lives, our children, and our friends to be so much more important than anyone else's.

Almost in every large crowd, we can find someone holding up a sign that reads John 3:16. That passage is held in front of us too. The message from Jesus is that God sent Him to save us, not to condemn us, because He so loved us. He did not just love the world. He so loved the world. God so loves us that He tells us to believe in the message of His Son. God so loves us that He wants us to share in eternal life. In our world, which seems over the top most days, we must learn to so love. We must pass on the message to our children, our families, our coworkers, and our communities. We must so love one another because He came not to condemn, but to so save us. God so loves us.

For everyone who does wicked things hates the light and does not come toward the light, so that his works might not be exposed. But whoever lives the truth comes to the light, so that his works may be clearly seen as done in God.

JOHN 3:20, 21

Secrets have no place in our Christian lives. Whispering can only cause suspicion and anxiety. I had an employee once who whispered all the time. She whispered to the other employees, which made customers wonder if she was talking about them. She whispered to the customers, which made me wonder if she had something to tell the customers that she did not want the rest of us to hear. She whispered on the phone to friends and was always "stirring the pot." Secrets are kept in the dark. They have no place in our families or our businesses or our communities.

Jesus tells us that what is done behind our backs, in the dark, is not to be given recognition. We have the power to teach our children and others to walk in the light. We have the power to teach them to share their stories so they will shine brightly in the truth of the living Christ. When we live in truth, we have no secrets. Our lives are open to the love of Jesus Christ, and we can openly share that love. Light your candle and spread the light of Christ, the light of truth so that all may see clearly the works of Jesus. Come to the Light.

"If you knew the gift of God and who is saying to you, 'Give me a drink,' you would have asked him and he would have given you living water."

JOHN 4:10

Many times in my life I have said, "If I only knew." I wish I had known my child was going to get an award at the banquet. If only I had known, I would have canceled my appointment and attended. I wish I had known there was going to be a retreat this weekend so I could have ordered more pins. I wish I had known they were coming to town — I would have planned dinner. Truth is I could have known if I truly listened, if I used the gifts, if I had wanted to serve, if I asked, if I was willing to give.

Jesus speaks directly to us when He says, "If you knew." How many times have we said after the fact, "Well, if I knew it would help or there was going to be prizes or you really needed me?" Jesus speaks of living water. Living water does not sit stagnant in a pool. It flows. As God's gift continues to flow so must our faith. We are called to walk with eyes wide open and to be aware of all who ask for something, not to run ourselves all over and "do it all," but to simply take opportunities. On any given day we could tend to the very need that awards life eternal. If we knew.

January 19

"Everyone who drinks this water will be thirsty again; but whoever drinks the water I shall give will never thirst; the water I shall give will become in him a spring of water welling up to eternal life."

JOHN 4:13, 14

Lourdes, France, 1985. I stand amongst the thousands of people gathered in the exact place where a young girl, Bernadette Souborious, was visited by the Blessed Mother. A message from God was sent to this small, remote village, and that message was questioned and rejected, and the persistent messenger interrogated, until finally the spring of water that welled up cured. I stood in awe at the believers and wondered how many times God would send a message before we would actually obey. Sounds familiar. Message sent by God to a young girl and the spring that wells up cures and then those who witness the miracles believe. I drank the water and I saw the cures and I believed, but blessed are those who do not see and yet believe that Jesus Christ is the water, the One who will sustain us, who will quench us, and in Him we will be brought to eternal life.

Jesus offers us eternal life. We're thinking He wants us to drink from the well that is right in front of us, but then we realize that He wants us to go much deeper. He comes to us, and He sends others to us to remind us that He alone can save us. He reminds us that

He is that water, and the more we believe, the more we take in and the more our own spring wells up and flows. Like the Samaritan woman, like Bernadette, we must take Him into our lives and allow Him to overflow into the lives of others. He sustains.

"But the hour is coming, and is now here, when true worshipers will worship the Father in Spirit and truth; and indeed the Father seeks such people to worship him. God is Spirit and those who worship him must worship in Spirit and truth."

JOHN 4:23, 24

Sought after. This brings to mind Francis Thompson's famous poem, "The Hound of Heaven." I'm sure there are many interpretations, but most seem to point to the simple fact that our God is in constant pursuit of us. Although we may seek fulfillment in the ways of this world, God "hounds" us to lead lives that will bring us to Him. It is an awesome feeling for someone to seek us out. Maybe we know something they'd like to know or have a talent they would like to learn or benefit from or simply they'd like to spend some time with us. No matter the reason for someone to actively seek us, it gives us a nice feeling.

We can certainly feel good because the Father Himself seeks us. Jesus tells us that the hour is now. We are called this moment to worship in Spirit and in truth. He wants to spend time with us. He wants us to worship Him because He knows that we are people of faith, and He knows that we are true to Him, and by our example others will come to believe and worship the truth. The Father seeks us.

"I am he, the one who is speaking with you."

JOHN 4:26

Growing up, we loved to watch the TV show *To Tell the Truth*. As the show began, three different people stood in the dark, and as the light shown on each they would announce that they were the same person. "I'm Paul Packer," each would say. Then, the contestant would ask each one questions to try to figure out which person was truly Paul Packer. I loved that show. The writers made it all seem so mysterious. And who doesn't like to figure out a good mystery? We love to be the first to know the answer because we love to be the first to tell.

The disciples are "amazed" that Jesus is talking to a woman when they return. But who else? Who else could He have chosen who would tell the entire town that the Messiah has come? Jesus probably knew that this woman would first and foremost believe Him and that she would immediately go out and tell others. He speaks to us today. He tells us today that He is the one. Jesus is the one who even knowing everything about us, has come to save us. Each and every day, He comes and He is here for us. The woman knows that One is coming who will "tell us everything" and now here He has come and He can handle our everything. We must go out, leave our water jars, drop what we're doing, tell the truth, and spread the word. He is speaking to us.

January 22

"I have food to eat of which you do not know."

JOHN 4:32

I am not much on going out to lunch while I'm at work. Salesmen coming to our store know they will have my husband join them because, being diabetic, he has to eat, but also he's just a nice guy. I wish I could say that I substitute my lunch for something positive, but I generally just eat a sandwich or peanut butter snack crackers from home and sip a Coke. Can we imagine what others would say if we told them "No thanks. We're not going to lunch today. We have our own source of nourishment." They would all want to know if we're on a diet or what sort of hidden treats we have or if we are sick. We might feed a different hunger this way. We could go to a noon Mass or read a spiritual book or visit someone in the hospital or serve at a soup kitchen.

Jesus does not talk to us about physical food. The food He speaks about is that which nourishes Him because He is doing the will of the Father. He speaks about taking a break from our normal routine. No one needs to know or understand. In turn, we will satisfy, and we can be satisfied. Choose that which nourishes.

"They can no longer die, for they are like angels; and they are the children of God because they are the ones who will rise."

LUKE 20:36

There is comfort in the resurrection. I could not imagine not believing there is more than this life and we die and that's all. I have a little brother, Frank Gerard, who only lived a few days before he died from complications because of a hole in his heart. I have a big brother who died at thirty-three. I have best friends who died well before they had the best years of their lives. Thank You, Lord, that there is so much more and they are like angels and they are the children of God.

Jesus assures us that we have loved ones, like angels, who are children of God. His resurrection opened the way for those who die before us to be welcomed into a place far greater than we have here. We pray for all who have gone before us that they may rise, and if they have already reached that glorious place, we ask that they pray for us. Through the mercy of God.

"The reaper is already receiving his payment and gathering crops for eternal life, so that the sower and reaper can rejoice together."

JOHN 4:36

In my mind, I am constantly comparing myself to others and wondering what they're doing that I'm not doing. I cannot help it. I want to know why they're smiling all the time, how they have time to attend Bible studies and visit the sick and take meals to a family whose parent just died. How do they have time for all their works of mercy when I rarely have time to work my mercy with my family and my coworkers? Am I jealous of the time others have to "gather crops"? Am I jealous that their payment could be that they are joyful, happy people? Done with good intentions, all our work can edge us towards eternal life. I think about parents doing everyday tasks for their families and teachers working the same problems over and over, employees dealing with coworkers' constant mistakes and neighbors working together for a better community, a better world. Our simple daily routines can "gather crops," can receive instant "payment" when done with complete, unconditional love.

Jesus confirms that He came to save us. He came to give us examples, to sow the seed. He tells us straight forward that we can reap the benefits of all He has done for us. He tells us that through our lives, our everyday normal lives, we can work toward eternal life, and some day we will rejoice with Him. Jesus loves us, and He has given us the natural instincts to show compassion and to care for others and to lead with kindness and to share love. Our attitude alone toward our children, our spouses, our work, our neighbors, our brothers, and our sisters can prove to be a gathering of crops. Reap what He has sown so today, and forever we can rejoice. Together.

January 25

"I sent you to reap what you have not worked for; others have done the work, and you are sharing the fruits of their work."

JOHN 4:38

My family flat out benefits from the years of work my parents have done. We are beyond grateful to them for all they have done for us. Just the same, we know that others can benefit from our hard work or we hope they do. We can count ourselves on the opposite end of Christ's words today. We cook, we clean, we coach, we serve at church, at work, and in our communities. The people around us are constantly reaping from all we do.

Jesus tells us to take notice of all those who have prepared our way. Be grateful for our stove, our oven, and our microwave instead of expecting a pat on the back for a nice dinner. Be grateful for our washing machine and dryer instead of complaining about the piles of laundry. Be thankful for the car that drove us to the church to serve, the bus and the driver that got us to work, and even the zip lock bag that kept our sandwich fresh until we had time for lunch. Someone before us has used their God given talents so that what we have to do may be done more efficiently. Jesus calls us to be grateful for those who have made our lives a little easier today. There are many.

"Amen, I say to you, in no one in Israel have I found such faith."

MATTHEW 8:10

I love to put myself in the Gospel passage. Today, I am standing there next to this guy and I have known him for what I feel is forever. I am shocked at his belief in Jesus. To me, he's always been the authority figure, telling us all what to do. Yet today he humbles himself right in front of me and everyone. Because of his belief, the man says his servant will be healed, and within an hour he is well. I'm completely awed by his deep faith.

Jesus calls us to be unrecognizable in our faith. He teaches us that even when we think we know someone, we should never assume we do. Even when we think we know ourselves, He may turn things around. When we humble ourselves before God, He can quiet a crowd. When we have faith, like no one else, He can heal. He wants us to put ourselves in the Gospel message and learn deep faith. Like no other.

"Amen, I say to you, no prophet is accepted in his own native place."

LUKE 4:24

C oming off a retreat, a lecture, a homily, a minute of spiritual direction, the type that gives us the huge smack on the forehead, that feeling of eureka!, is difficult to explain, especially to those closest to us. We tend to get the reaction "Oh great! Mom's at it again" or "Here we go again with the Holy Spirit thing." People who know us best find it most difficult to believe when we've had a spiritual change, a holy eureka. They've seen our craziness, and they know our previous language, our habits. Who are we to suddenly share anything about Jesus?

Today we get the big eureka! Oh, this is why I "got it" when someone else told me the same thing my mother had been telling me for years. Oh, this is why my kids roll their eyes with me, but the minute their grandparent says the same thing it becomes the "Gospel." Jesus knows. He's been there. He knows from personal experience that the job will not be easy. He knows what it means to humble ourselves, to have others think we're going off the deep end, and yet He still expects us to share the Good News, and He wants us to start in our own back yards. If we have found the secret to a better life, a cure for diabetes, anything that made our quality of life better, wouldn't we want to share it, especially with those closest to us? Share the Spirit, the eureka moments, despite the rejections. Jesus speaks directly to us.

January 28

"Unless you people see signs and wonders, you will not believe."

JOHN 4:48

I had never journeyed with a large group on pilgrimage before I traveled to Medjugorje. Before I knew it, I was meeting a plane full of people from all over the U.S. with matching luggage tags. All in search of the signs and wonders and messages Our Lady was giving in a small remote place thousands of miles from our homes. We traveled by large plane, by small plane, by bus, and by car. We prayed and we sang and we walked and we talked and we finally arrived in a tiny, remote village. The faith of my fellow pilgrims that we would even survive the trip was wonder enough for me, but what would come over the next couple of days proved greater. My mom and I watched and listened as old and young packed the small church to attend Mass and pray the Rosary. Our group went to talk to one of the visionaries, and we climbed the hill to the cross, helping others along the way, witnessing the faith of those in bare feet on sharp slate. We listened to stories of rosaries turning from silver to gold, and we watched from outside through the stain glass of the church as the visionaries spoke with Mary in the choir loft. Signs and wonders, documented or not, bringing people from all over the world to believe.

Jesus says that He understands we need signs and wonders, and so He performs them. But we have to be open to them, to listen, follow, believe. How many times does He have to send His Mother with the message to repent, to fast, and to pray? What more do we have to see? Roses in winter, curing water, dancing sun? We are called today to see the signs and wonders. And to believe.

"This is the time of fulfillment. The kingdom of God is at hand. Repent, and believe in the gospel."

MARK 1:15

At age eight, a friend and I decided to attend Saturday morning Mass. We went a couple of Saturdays in a row, and each time we noticed that everyone there was much older than us. They were more our parents age or older, so we decided that we had plenty of time to "do all those things" later and stopped going. I've always had the idea that I'd get closer to Jesus when I got older. I'd wait and do all the "extras" later that might give me a more personal relationship with the Lord. Go to daily Mass, take time for Eucharistic Adoration, learn to pray the Liturgy of the Hours, obtain the promises of the Sacred Heart, and the list could go on and on. Our faith is incredibly rich with traditional ways to come closer to Jesus and with opportunities to deepen that relationship. Whether we're eight or eighteen, thirty-eight or eighty-eight, the kingdom is at hand and the opportunity to enjoy the riches of that kingdom lay before us.

Jesus says that today is the day. The time is now, and the more we take the time, the more time He will give. As we read and write and pray and celebrate and attend to the details of furthering our love for Him, we become aware of something more fulfilling. We begin to live a joy filled life in Christ, who is our joy. We are never too young and never too old. Listen to Him. Ask forgiveness and believe in the Word. He speaks to us.

"Come after me, and I will make you fishers of men."

MATTHEW 4:19

We are called to many professions in life. We are parents and teachers, doctors, lawyers, dentists, waitresses, secretaries, CEOs, engineers, and real estate agents. We work in news rooms and office buildings, stores, airports, and hospitals. We lead, we nurture, we console, we listen, we respond, and we love. We turn heads, turn our cheeks, and turn things around. We make a difference. If we stop and think about our day, we come into contact with hundreds of people. Inside my house, it starts with seven people, then on to school and work and the grocery. The telephone and the Internet add on quite a few. Each morning we must ask Jesus to help us make a difference in someone out of those hundred. The way we treat one another, the patience we show, the time we give, the tone in our voice, the smile on our face, and the touch of our hands can all make a difference.

Jesus calls us to come after Him and fish. Put on our waders or climb in the boat, bait the hook, and cast the line. Some will take the bait and run and others will be reeled in. Many will fish alongside us. Jesus calls us from our professions to a higher position. Sitting in patience and in persistence. In our busy lives, often the most difficult part is being still and waiting. But we are all called to be fishers of men. Follow Him. Fish.

January 31

"Be quiet! Come out of him!"

LUKE 4:35

One of my favorite lines from my mother is "you're just talking to hear yourself talk." With eight of us kids trying to tell her things at the same time, I am sure there were many days when she could not "hear herself think." I have always loved to talk. Being number six of eight, I had to talk a lot to get a "word in edgewise." My mom would suggest "listen to yourself sometime" or "count to ten before you speak." Being truly quiet is difficult. In conversations we catch ourselves speaking before others have finished because we think maybe what we have to say is more important or will just help move the conversation along. It's not easy in this hectic world to truly listen. Listening takes practice.

Jesus exclaims "Be quiet!" Listen. He has the answer. He is the answer. He is the cure. Shhh. Hear His words. He can fix your life. Make it better. Go to Him. Sit in silence. He wants us to quiet our minds and our hearts and let out whatever it is inside us that keeps us from Him. Count to ten slowly and often. Be quiet.

"Put out into deep water and lower your nets for a catch."

LUKE 5:4

y uncles were great fishermen. They knew how to catch the "big ones," and if they didn't, they always had a wild tale about the one that got away. Hands spread wider and wider to explain sizes as their stories got deeper and deeper. Their father loved to take them fishing. It was where they spent time together and shared stories. They, in turn, took time with their boys. And so on. Nothing better each year than a family gathering at a fish fry. It was one more reason to gather us all together and share great stories.

Jesus calls us to go to the depths, to the deepest parts, to the darkest areas. He calls us to take time with the poorest, the hungriest, and the dirtiest. He wants us to lower ourselves to be present to the most obnoxious coworker, the most difficult student, the nosiest neighbor, the most negative family member. He wants us to go deeper, to share our stories and to let others share theirs' so that we can all come to Him. He calls us to take time, to lower our nets, and as we catch, others will catch on. It is one more reason to gather us all together. Take the chance. Go out.

"Do not be afraid; from now on you will be catching men."

LUKE 5:10

o not be afraid." I loved hearing this every time Bl. Pope John Paul II spoke it, especially to our young people. He knew above all else that our youth, if caught early enough, could spread Christianity better than anyone. Young people have less awareness of fear. Young people have a simple innocence that is believable. Young people don't hold back on what they believe. It is important today to teach our young girls to be modest and chaste. It is important to teach our young boys to be gentlemen. Yes, there are cool clothes that cover, and no, not everyone is doing it. Yes, they can be kind and gentle and still be manly. Our young people, our young girls, our young boys, can set the pace. They are our leaders.

Jesus came to us as a baby. He taught in the temple as a young boy. He knew the truth and was not afraid to teach and to preach, to tell stories and to spread Christianity. No fear. We will have many times when we feel we are alone in this mission of Jesus, when it would be easier just to give in to all of the temptations of this world. But what has this world to offer? Jesus offers happiness, peace, joy, and everlasting life. Do not be afraid.

"I do will it. Be made clean."

MARK 1:41

Making things clean reminds me of the huge, baldheaded "Mr. Clean," who stood with hands on hips before the most sparkling clean floors I'd ever seen on TV or anywhere else. He never worked in our house enough for me to see myself in the floors. But we were big into covering up the unsightly blots and blemishes of our lives. Ink spots on our favorite shirt, water stains on wood, brown age spots, wall cracks; you name it, we could shout it out, sand it, paint it, cover it up, hide it or patch it and no one would know there was ever a flaw — except us.

Jesus however tells us that at His will, all is made clean. We may "shout out" the toughest stains, but Jesus says no shouting, no scrubbing, or spraying or soaking is necessary. He is calm, and He is clear. Be made clean because it is simply His will. Seems easy, but we still must do it. We still must come to Him, as the leper did, in our brokenness, in our imperfection, in our dirt, in our stain, with our blots and our blemishes, and we can be made clean. Not a cover up, but a complete cleansing, inside and out. Take a deep breath. Jesus wills it. He is in charge. Be made clean.

"What are you thinking in your hearts? Which is easier, to say, 'Your sins are forgiven,' or to say, 'Rise and walk'? But that you may know that the Son of Man has authority on earth to forgive sins ... "I say to you, rise, pick up your stretcher, and go home."

LUKE 5:22–24

My mother spent several thousand dollars one year to have an expert come to our business and teach me how to manage a successful store without physically doing all the work myself. At the time, I was going into work early, leaving late, and taking work home with me. Basically, he taught me how to delegate, how to let go, how to work with others without feeling the need to be in control of everything; how to trust others to do their job well. Now, I have more time at work to spend talking with customers and coworkers and more time at home with family. Expert advice freed me to act with authority.

Jesus speaks to us today and frees us from any tension we may feel of being in control. God gave Him the authority, not us. We are drawn to not just a physical healing, but a spiritual healing as well. He tells us to rise and pick up whatever it is that holds us down and go home to a place of rest and peacefulness. Expert advice. He's got us. We do not need to do everything. Let go.

February 5

"Those who are well do not need a physician, but the sick do. Go and learn the meaning of the words, 'I desire mercy, not sacrifice.' I did not come to call the righteous but sinners."

MATTHEW 9:12, 13

I will never forget my son's Reconciliation night. He was so happy, and he wanted me to share the same happiness. He suggested some great ideas for me to confess to one of the priests. He assured me I only really had to choose three sins to confess. Others would need some time too. The last time I had received the Sacrament of Reconciliation, I was seven months pregnant with this child. Seven years without formally confessing. Who am I to think that I don't need the great Physician; that I am perfect? When I did finally sit with this young priest, this instrument, I could feel the Holy Spirit lift the weight of sin and righteousness right off my shoulders. I felt an amazing change deep inside.

Jesus calls us this day to get over ourselves. He knows the ways of the world, the temptations, and yet, He beckons us to His mercy. He's been here. He lived among our sinfulness and overcame the same temptations we face every day. He is here. He knows the difficulties, the pains, and the hardships. He knows it all to the point of dying to make a better place for us. Admit it. Ask for His mercy and get on with a better life. Be healed.

"Can the wedding guests fast while the bridegroom is with them? As long as they have the bridegroom with them they cannot fast. But the days will come when the bridegroom is taken away from them, and then they will fast on that day."

MARK 2:19, 20

I'm not really good at fasting in the sense of going without food to specifically empty myself to allow more room for the Spirit to dwell. I do know that fasting allows us to open ourselves more fully to God; to humble ourselves before Him. Fasting provides an emptiness that can be filled with a new relationship with Jesus Christ. But I think many of us go without whether intentionally or not. We give second helpings to our kids and forego eating a full plate ourselves. We give up our personal time to tutor a student. We deny ourselves a break to allow a coworker a little extra time for a special situation or we listen a little longer when we want to be doing something else.

Jesus tells us to take time with one another. He says that there will be plenty of time for traditional fasting and that He wants us to be with Him and to be with others at the Feast of life. He calls us to celebrate this moment; this fresh new message of Resurrection and new life. He is in our midst. Let us not deny ourselves.

"No one patches an old cloak with a piece of unshrunken cloth, for its fullness pulls away from the cloak and the tear gets worse. People do not put new wine into old wineskins. Otherwise the skins burst, the wine spills out, and the skins are ruined. Rather, they pour new wine into fresh wineskins, and both are preserved."

MATTHEW 9:16, 17

*W*hen I moved into my home, I hired a young man to remove an aluminum roof from our back patio and transform a plain concrete slab into a beautiful screened porch. After two years I noticed that each rain brought a little more water through the roof of the porch. I would climb out of my child's bedroom window each summer and patch the problems. For five summers, I bent metal, I caulked, and I spread black goop between shingles. Temporary fixes. Finally my brother sent several workmen to replace the roof. I watched them methodically cut into the side of the house. One of the men showed me where the years of a leaking roof had damaged the inside area over our den. They replaced the rotted wood and built a new roof for my patio. No leaks, no patching.

Jesus calls us to stop patching the areas of our lives that need work. He does not want us to simply mend things because temporary fixes can often make things worse. He wants us to take the time to do His work right. Pull it all out and fix it properly. Start from scratch if we have to because He has great things for those who go about life the right way. Constant patching is getting us nowhere. Take some time. Fix it right. Persevere.

February 8

"Look, you are well; do not sin any more, so that nothing worse may happen to you."

JOHN 5:14

We really do not have time to be sick. That's the way most of us feel. Someone needs us. Our parents, our aunt, our children, our coworker or our neighbor need our faithful assistance. But life does not always work the way we want it to work. Once, in the middle of the night, I woke with an excruciating pain in my side. I found it difficult to breathe. My oldest daughter took me to the hospital and we found out that I had infection in one lung. I thought I had broken a rib. The doctor gave me pain medicine and pumped me full of antibiotics, and for three days I did not know or care too much about what was going on in my world. I was of no use to anyone. I could not even pray.

Jesus tells us under no uncertain terms that He wants us well. He confirms that the world will trample right past us day after day, but with Him all things are possible. We can also hear Him say clearly, now do not sin anymore. He knows full well that when we sin, we are in a weakened condition. We are vulnerable. We are open to the world, and we do not have time for what the world has to offer; all the trampling. When we are well, we are much more capable of meeting the challenges of this world. When we are fully charged, we can bring others closer to the only one who can make us well. Allow the healing. Stay strong.

February 9

"My Father is at work until now, so I am at work."

JOHN 5:17

Our lives are constant. As I was working late one night, my sister Jeanne called wondering why I was not at home. I explained that I was trying to finish my work, and her response has stayed with me since, "Don't you know we never finish. We just have to stop at some point and leave it. It'll be there tomorrow. Go home." And once home, more work, but it was home.

Jesus speaks to us. He reminds us every day that He is at work in us so that we may continue the work of the Father and the Son with the Holy Spirit. Just as Mary's "yes" changed the world, our "yes" to the daily work of our vocations can and will make a difference. As parents raising children, as children obeying parents, as those called to prayer and fasting or passing on the faith, as those called to single life or married life, as old or as young, we as Christians are called to make such an impact in our work that others remember Jesus Christ. No matter what our calling in life, God calls each of us to be faithful, to be strong examples to our families and our communities and our world. Be at His work.

February 10

"Amen, amen, I say to you, a son cannot do anything on his own, but only what he sees his father doing; for what he does, his son will do also. For the Father loves his Son and shows him everything that he himself does, and he will show him greater works than these, so that you may be amazed."

JOHN 5:19, 20

Good examples. My older sisters have been my examples all through my life. Trying to keep up with those two made for a busy childhood. I played every sport I could find, rode horses, was a cheerleader, attended retreats, danced and sang with our youth organization, and ran for leadership offices in school. I never questioned, never hesitated. They participated, and so I did. They had fun, and so I did.

Jesus speaks to us about the importance of being examples to one another. As Christians, we should be more than just the voice spreading the word. We should be examples of Christ's compassion, His perseverance, His love, and His tender heart. Jesus emulates His Father in His love and His mercy and His compassion, and in turn He asks that we mirror those qualities to everyone we meet so that they in turn will be His image to others. Good examples can help to change the world. Live each day in His image, and His greater works will amaze. Lead by His example.

 *February 11*

"Amen, amen, I say to you, whoever hears my word and believes in the one who sent me has eternal life and will not come to condemnation, but has passed from death to life."

JOHN 5:24

I can listen to people talk to me all day long. I listen while I am trying to take a nap, while I am cooking, while I am on the phone, while driving, and while busy at work. I cannot tell you how many times I have heard my child say, "Mom, I already told you that." "Mom, I asked you if I could go." "Mom, you said you wouldn't mind." I listened, but I never heard a word. I listened and responded, but I couldn't recall the conversation. The world is a busy place.

Jesus calls us to hear. Not to listen to His word, but to hear His word and to believe. He knows our ability to multi-task. Jesus knows our world is noisy and cluttered. He says to us that if we hear and believe, we will have eternal life. We have to take the time to clear the distractions, to stop what we're doing, to quiet ourselves and not just listen to the sounds of His voice, but to hear Him. In our busy world, believe and receive eternal life. Hear.

 *February 12*

"Amen, amen, I say to you, the hour is coming and is now here when the dead will hear the voice of the Son of God, and those who hear will live.

For just as the Father has life in himself, so also he gave to his Son the possession of life in himself."

*W*e stand right in the midst of the apostles and we hear Jesus say things that seem like they do not pertain to this world. We cannot understand His words. The pieces of the puzzle do not fit into the lives we are standing in at the time. The words are very confusing. I have sat through many, many classes and thought exactly the same thing. What is he saying? How will I ever use this lesson? Why did someone sign me up for this class? How can this pertain to my life? What hour is coming and now is here?

Jesus makes it easy for us to see that we are the lucky ones. We see the word as it was given after the Resurrection. Everything Jesus said as He stood in the midst of the apostles makes much more sense now, and isn't it great to know that there is so much more? Jesus Christ came so that we can live. He tells us that even if we are in denial, even if we are dead to what God has to offer, He still has something to say. He pertains to our life. He is the lesson. Hear and live.

February 13

"I cannot do anything on my own; I judge as I hear, and my judgment is just, because I do not seek my own will but the will of the one who sent me."

I love to be independent. I prefer to do things on my own. I have managed to hurt my back more times than I can count, to spend an afternoon with a dresser stuck in a staircase, to sit stranded on a roof waiting for help with a ladder and to scratch the side of my husband's truck with a Christmas tree. I tend to get myself into "situations" before I admit that I need help. God did not make me strong enough on purpose. I cannot just will things to work. He wants me to work with others, to need help, to humble myself to ask, to be patient, and to wait.

Jesus comes right out and says that He cannot do anything on His own. And He tells us that, yes, we are strong, and we have many gifts, but we cannot go through life without Him. We are given all the positive possibilities to change the world over to Christ because we know deep in our hearts that we need another. The message may take a hard turn every now and then, but we get it. We accept that we cannot do anything on our own, especially His will, and that acceptance empowers us to be examples in the world. Let go of it all. Let God work through us.

"But I have testimony greater than John's. The works that the Father gave me to accomplish, these works that I perform testify on my behalf that the Father has sent me. Moreover, the Father who sent me has testified on my behalf. But you have never heard his voice nor seen his form, and you do not have his word remaining in you, because you do not believe in the one whom he has sent."

JOHN 5:36–38

I enjoy reading or listening to the testimonies of those who have been truly touched by Jesus in their lives. I have attended many men's conferences, women's conferences, priest retreats, mom retreats, book talks, speeches, and panels. Some speakers share a change in their lives that make a huge impact on those around them and others are changed just for their own families. Either way, all have these testimonies to share because they were open to the encounter they have had with Jesus. Jesus was sent to us with works to accomplish, and He is here now to have us be His voice and His hands and His feet and His ears.

Jesus tells us that all He has come to do is to accomplish the works of His Father. He calls us to be open to those works. He calls us to perform on His behalf. The more we work in His name, the better the performance. And we all love a grand performance. He wants us to share. He wants us to be open to testify. We are sent.

"You search the scriptures, because you think you have eternal life through them; even they testify on my behalf. But you do not want to come to me to have life."

JOHN 5:39, 40

I am constantly in search of something better. I look for the "good life" in the world and am left bored and depressed, so I go shopping. I have a rough day at work or with the kids, so I take a nap. I get tired of searching in my world and need a break, so I take a vacation. When I come back from shopping or wake from my nap or as I unpack from my vacation, I realize quickly that the world I escaped is right where I left it. I am temporarily relieved and my search begins all over again. Magazines, the Internet, catalogs, books … I read and study and search, but it all just leads to more searching.

Jesus says that if we want the "real thing," the great parts of life that last forever, we should stop searching through this world to find them. To have life, we must go to Him for everything. He will take us when we are tired, depressed, and lonely or excited, overjoyed, and overwhelmed. Scripture confirms that to have life, we must have Jesus. In Him, our joy is complete. Go to Him. Visit. Take time.

February 16

"I do not accept human praise; moreover, I know that you do not have the love of God in you. I came in the name of my Father, but you do not accept me; yet if another comes in his own name, you will accept him."

JOHN 5:41–43

When we read a book or an article by a certain author that excites us or we listen to a speaker that motivates or moves us, we want to share the names with everyone. We love to pass along a great message. We had a parish priest come to our bookstore for an autograph party, and I wish everybody in the diocese could have heard him speak. His stories, his enthusiasm for the Gospel, and his love for his vocation were motivating. After he finished, I jumped on the Internet and told everyone who would take the time to read about his incredible witness to the faith. I wanted others to feel the same satisfaction, the same good feeling that those who heard him felt.

Jesus wants us to accept Him and spread His news just the same as we jump on the bandwagon of a good book or a motivating speaker. He could say to us, "Why do you think these people have the capabilities to motivate and to give such satisfaction? I gave them those gifts." But He says instead that it is not human praises He's after from us. He simply wants us to accept His teachings in the name of His Father. We can see His power through others and we can motivate others to accept His message. Share His name with everyone.

"How can you believe, when you accept praise from one another and do not seek the praise that comes from the only God? Do not think that I will accuse you before the Father: the one who will accuse you is Moses, in whom you have placed your hope."

JOHN 5:44, 45

We like the approval of others. We enjoy that "pat on the back" for a job well done or a tough effort. We suspect something's wrong when we don't receive praise in our jobs, with our projects, for our children's behavior, as we strive to be good Christians, hard workers, and good parents, holy people, and strong witnesses to the faith. We know we shouldn't need praise for the small acts we do each day, but it is nice. It's nice to be noticed. It's nice to have confirmation.

Jesus tells us not to worry about criticism or judgment or praise except that which comes from God. Easier said than done in this world. But if we truly live only to please God, to be praised by Him, we could be bolder in our actions and truthful in our speech and our stomachs would not be in knots worrying about who approves and how we measure up. God's stamp of approval, in our every day, is all we need. He is our pat on the back for a job well done. He notices.

"For if you had believed Moses, you would have believed me, because he wrote about me. But if you do not believe his writings, how will you believe my words?"

JOHN 5:46, 47

A wonderful study for my own spiritual life was reviewing the Ten Commandments with my second grader. He brought home worksheets that sketched out how each commandment pertains to our lives. For instance, this second grader certainly wasn't going to kill anyone, but the worksheet went on to ask whether he had ever hurt someone's chances to make new friends by talking badly about them. Did he mistreat others or hurt their reputation or character? As we listen to our children, do we simply agree with them or do we call for them to act with charity and forgiveness? As we climb "the ladder of success," do we step on anyone? Can we go an entire day without saying one thing that may kill a reputation?

Jesus tells us to believe. Believe Moses' writings and believe His words. We are to follow the depths of the commandments. As Christians, we may be the only Gospel that reaches another. We are the example that others follow. He wants us to live His teachings as Moses wrote and He preached. Believe and live.

February 19

"The sabbath was made for man, not man for the sabbath."

MARK 2:27

*E*xtended hours. For several years during December, we opened our bookstore on Sundays for those who were unable to shop during the week. We thought it good to give everyone the opportunity to purchase religious gifts for Christmas. After all…blah, blah, loads of reasoning. I worked for six or seven days a week non-stop until I heard a talk at a retreat that stressed that the importance of our day of rest was such that God had made a commandment about it. In this hectic world, we need a day of rest. I need a day of rest. I am not better than anyone else. I am not at my best without a break.

Jesus reiterates the importance of a day of rest. God created the seventh day for us. He knows that we cannot go seven days without rest and perform to our highest ability. We extend our hours and ourselves until soon there is nothing left but a frazzled, tired, over-extended somebody trying to do more with less. Listen to His words. The Sabbath was created for us. Observe.

February 20

"Which one of you who has a sheep that falls into a pit on the sabbath will not take hold of it and lift it out? How much more valuable a person is than a sheep. So it is lawful to do good on the sabbath."

MATTHEW 12:11, 12

*R*ules taken to the extreme. I can think of several times at work and at home when to save a bigger mistake or a tragedy, a rule has been bent or broken. At our bookstore, we give no refunds without a receipt, unless there's a good reason. We never take samples from salespeople who just happen to come in the front door without a scheduled appointment. In our family, we never accept a ride home from school, unless the weather is surprisingly hazardous and we are good friends with the driver. Yes, my children have walked in the rain. Through it all, if something happens or if a person is upset or hurt, we can always count on someone responding, "but you said," "but the rule is," "but we're not supposed to." Now they decide to remember a rule!

Jesus gives us rules to follow, but He says that we should never allow harm to come to another just to follow a rule. He tells us that more important than any rule are the people around us. The answer is in our hearts. Keep the commandments. Do the right thing. And most importantly, know the value of the person and take care of one another. To the extreme.

February 21

"Blessed are the poor in spirit, / for theirs is the kingdom of heaven."
MATTHEW 5:3

When I made the retreat weekend called Cursillo, in my mind I was already full of all that could be given to me. I went because my mother signed me up. But I was full of information and knowledge and could answer questions at my assigned table and had so much to offer the other people in this building. Three days of this and I imagined that I would be bursting with pride of how much I could share about Jesus and our call here on this earth and our response to that call. By the second day, my throat was so tight, I literally could only speak at a whisper. I am allergic to feathers and although I'd brought my own pillow, the shelves above where I was sleeping were filled with old feather pillows. My voice was gone. While I listened, because that was all I could do, I myself was filled for the day and a half I had left with all that Jesus wanted me to hear. He literally shut me up to fill me up. I lay empty before all these women, and I was filled.

Jesus says that those who are aware of their own spiritual poverty, those who understand that they are nothing without Him, are those who are blessed. He has the gift of Heaven waiting for those who let go of their pride and depend solely on Him. We empty ourselves of our will and allow Him to fill us with His will. We are nothing without God. Let go.

"Blessed are they who mourn, / for they will be comforted."

MATTHEW 5:4

There are definitely many times in my life when I have felt that there is no comfort for my sadness. Most of them have been brought about by the death of a loved one; my brother, my nephew, my friends, my golf partner, my grandparents, my uncle, my cousin, my in-laws. On the other hand, sadness also has been due to a different kind of loss; a break in a relationship with friends or siblings or parents. Relationships are tough. No one ever said they'd be easy, and to work they constantly have to be worked on. We have to learn to give with the take. We do not like to be at odds with others. We naturally like everyone to get along and act right. And so we should be with Jesus.

Jesus says that those who are sad about the break in their relationship with Him are blessed. As we are truly sorry for our sins, for our failures to others, He is here to comfort us. He is here to make things better, and with Him all is well. We regret the times when our relationship with Him is strained due to sin. We desire things to be better, and Jesus tells us that as we mourn the loss of Him, He is with us. He will never leave us. Through whatever peaks and valleys our relationship may wander, He is in it for the long haul. Jesus comforts. Jesus remains.

"Blessed are the meek, / for they will inherit the land."

MATTHEW 5:5

We like to be in control. We like for our children to be well behaved, our homes to be well put together, our dinners prepared, our businesses successful, and our lives to run smoothly, and we like to be the ones to orchestrate it all. Truth is, we are often left feeling overworked, stressed, unappreciated, and too tired to ever enjoy all our blessings. In my day, I pack multiple lunches, run a couple of loads of laundry, get children ready for school, fix breakfast, get myself ready for work, drive children to school, go to work with my husband, buy, sell, talk, listen, pay bills, pick children up from school, help with homework, make dinner, run a load of laundry, clean the kitchen, and put children to bed. It took my mom many years to convince me that meek is not weak; that if I would allow Jesus to order my day, all will be well. I still do just as much, but I wake up an hour earlier and offer it all into His hands. I wouldn't say I'm not stressed at times, but I would say that somehow, it all gets done a little easier and I have time to enjoy my husband and my children and my work when I let Him be in control.

Jesus tells us that those who allow Him to take control of their lives will find harmony in the world around them. We can have a life of security and contentment if we let go of self and permit Jesus to take over. Let go and let God!

February 24

"Blessed are they who hunger and thirst for righteousness, / for they will be satisfied."

MATTHEW 5:6

We love satisfaction. When we read on a product label, "satisfaction guaranteed," we are more apt to buy because we know that we can return the item if we are not completely satisfied. We constantly look for ways to be satisfied; new clothes, a special vacation, a party, time alone, a pay increase. And yet, even when we think we can be satisfied by worldly goods or the option to return them, how long does the feeling last? For most of us, it just prompts us to look for the next thing that will satisfy.

Jesus tells us that we who continuously desire what is right, will be satisfied. When we desire what is moral and ethical and virtuous, we conform to His will. Because He dwells within us, our greatest needs, what we hunger for the most, are satisfied, taken care of, quenched. Jesus Christ is constantly in our hearts and in our souls and on our minds. Righteousness is Jesus Christ. Satisfaction guaranteed.

February 25

"Blessed are the merciful, / for they will be shown mercy."

MATTHEW 5:7

The Corporal and Spiritual Works of Mercy stand before us in our everyday routine. We feed, we clothe, we visit, we instruct, we comfort. We are a compassionate group. We care how others feel about us. We want everyone to get along with one another in our families and in our businesses and in our communities. We want people to be nice and play fair. It is important for us to take care of one another on this earth. I watch countless parents each year at our schools take time to send out emails for sick teachers or students, send food for families who have experienced a death, and provide time to care for classes and volunteer in the lunchroom. They give, give, give, while I use the excuse of work. Be careful to care. Sometimes the little things in life, a funeral home visit, a card sent, words of kindness or a phone call can make a difference.

Jesus tells us to take the time to show mercy. Take the opportunities set before us in our parking lot, in our house, in our neighborhood, in our school, and in our workplace. There are no chance encounters. We can learn a lot about ourselves from a pesky street person, a pain for a neighbor or a mean coworker. And, they can learn about a true Christian. Be merciful.

 February 26

"Blessed are the clean of heart, / for they will see God."

MATTHEW 5:8

I can think of nothing better than the pure, untarnished love of a child. I stood in line to sign up my sixth child for kindergarten and noticed all the young girls in tennis skirts and cute outfits taking their children alongside me. My guess was they thought I was Julia's grandmother. Julia was proud though. She held my hand and called me mommy despite the difference in the purple, bumpy veins sticking out of my legs and the other moms' sleek, exercised calves. I immediately wished I had worn pants. But my child's love for me is pure. It's straight from the heart. And that is how she often tells me how she feels, "Mom, I love you with all my heart."

Jesus calls each of us to have a clean heart. He wants us to love one another despite our differences. Just as our children see past all the flaws we think we should cover up, we are asked to let it all go, in ourselves and in others. Love without conditions. Love with a clean heart.

"Blessed are the peacemakers, / for they will be called children of God."
MATTHEW 5:9

*P*lay nice. A natural desire for us is to want everyone to get along. We want our children to play fair. We want our workers to work well together. We want our world to be at peace. When I'm begging God for my children to be nice to one another, I close my eyes and cannot help but see the faces of children in war-torn countries, wishing, begging, pleading for the noise, the violence, to stop.

Jesus says to us that when we work for peace, we are blessed. Peace starts in our own hearts and in our own homes. We cannot give what we do not have. Peace is built one heart at a time. Blessed are we when we pass it on to our families, our workplace, our church, our schools, our neighborhood, and our country. Maybe someday, through deep prayer and sacrifice, we may close our eyes and see the faces of children in a world of peace. He does not say blessed are those who are peaceful. He wants us to be peacemakers; to spread peace, to teach peace, to imitate His love to one another. When we are tools through which peace is generated, we do His work. Pray and play nice.

"Blessed are they who are persecuted for the sake of righteousness, / for theirs is the kingdom of heaven."

MATTHEW 5:10

*D*aily I tell my children to stop teasing one another. I tell them to let whatever their brothers or their sisters do or say roll off their backs. I preach "be the better person." If they just wouldn't react to the looks or the comments, their brother would stop trying to irritate them. I have read countless stories of saints who have become saints not because of what they did but because of how they did not react in anger to what was done or said to them. Many stories end with the conversion of the persecutor. It's difficult to compare a simple fight between siblings with the plight of great saints, but right is right no matter how big the fight. If we learn how to react or not react in small matters, we will know what to do in the larger world.

Jesus calls us all to righteousness for His sake. He calls us to be examples of turning the other cheek, not to develop weakness in character, but to strengthen our love for Him. Jesus will not give us more than we can handle. No matter the size of the fight, He calls us to act and to react for His sake. For the sake of righteousness.

February 29

"Blessed are you when they insult you and persecute you and utter every kind of evil against you [falsely] because of me."

MATTHEW 5:11

*I*nsults. Truth is, this one is difficult for many of us. If I have a stone thrown at me, my first reaction would be to pick it up and throw it back even harder. I'm number six of eight children. I know how to take care of myself. I know how to make it sting. But maybe I could have taken care of problems a little gentler in my youth. I actually had someone tell me recently that she was afraid of me in high school. I was so sad to hear those words. I just loved to have a good time back then, and I never meant to strike fear. But I was loud and crazy and I guess that was taken the wrong way.

Jesus tells us our actions and reactions are all in vain if they are not done because of Him. People are fragile. They tend to take life harder than we expect. Jesus calls us to check ourselves and our intentions. People talk and insult because we act for our own rewards, for our own satisfaction. Pick up the stone and put it back in your pocket. Tone down. Lower your voice. Take the hit. Do everything because of Jesus.

March 1

"You are the salt of the earth. But if salt loses its taste, with what can it be seasoned?"

MATTHEW 5:13

*M*om's southern cooking recommended salt in most recipes. Whether a pinch or a dash or simply "salt to taste," the white magic was listed in the instructions. The pot of green beans already included a salty chunk of ham, and yet the salt shaker was still upturned over the pot during the "cook-down" process. The salt shaker held a prominent spot in the center of most southern kitchen tables as if there could never be enough already cooked in the meal. Salt preserves our food, but it also gives it flavor. Once it's out of the shaker, we can't even see the tiny white specks, but we can taste the difference they make in many dishes.

Jesus speaks to us at point blank range. He is clear. We are the salt of the earth. We are here to preserve the teachings He spread. We are here to make a difference. We are not necessarily even supposed to be seen, but we are to make an impression that gives this world flavor. We are asked to be readily available at all times. Preserve. Go make a difference.

March 2

"Nor do they light a lamp and then put it under a bushel basket; it is set on a lampstand, where it gives light to all in the house. Just so, your light must shine before others, that they may see your good deeds and glorify your heavenly Father."

MATTHEW 5:15, 16

My husband loves different kinds of flashlights. It is really unbelievable how many he has purchased over the years, and yet the minute the power goes out in the house, we either cannot find one or the ones we do find have such dim lights they are not of much use. The kids play games with them or use the batteries for other needs, forgetting to replace them. German spotlight is a neighborhood favorite game during the summer. With the kids dressed in all black, the brighter the flashlight, the better chance the person who is "it" has of catching another player. The good flashlights are often in high demand.

Jesus tells us to keep the light within ourselves shining brightly so that we can be examples to others in His name. If we cannot find our own way or are worn down, we are useless. Energy gained from our own Christian lives from the Eucharist and the Sacraments and the Scriptures allow us to shine before others. Keep your charge. Let your light shine. Be in high demand.

"Therefore, whoever breaks one of the least of these commandments and teaches others to do so will be called least in the kingdom of heaven. But whoever obeys and teaches these commandments will be called greatest in the kingdom of heaven."

MATTHEW 5:18–20

*I*n our home, my husband and I have certain rules we would like obeyed. Don't bounce the ball. Don't run. Don't stand on the furniture. And yet, we know how it all works. If the oldest sets the pace and obeys, we're good. But the minute one falters, they all fall like dominoes. One throws the ball. They all join in, and the lamp gets broken. One starts running, soon they're all laughing and chasing one another, and someone gets hurt. Suddenly, the one who started it all is the least favorite at the moment.

Jesus means what He says here in the strictest sense. We think that we are only responsible for ourselves, but Jesus says that others will follow. He is clear. Obey. Be an example. Be great in the kingdom so that when one starts and the rest follow, no one gets hurt, and all will enter. Teach others.

"But I say to you, whoever is angry with his brother will be liable to judgment, and whoever says to his brother, 'Raqa,' will be answerable to the Sanhedrin, and whoever says, 'You fool,' will be liable to fiery Gehenna."

MATTHEW 5:22

I just cannot tolerate my children getting angry with one another. Some days they only have one another to rely on so why would they anger the one person they may need? We all know people who are just angry. They are always looking for something or someone to blame their miserable life on, and they are no fun to be around. Their family eventually has the same gloom and doom attitude and they seem not to be able to simply get along with one another.

Jesus tells us that anger in any form toward another is no good and can only bring about doom. We understand that by our "brother" He means not just our family but our friends, our neighbors, and all in our communities. We can start in our family because if we truly love our sisters, our brothers, and our parents, the rest of our world hopefully will follow by example. No name calling. No hatred. No anger towards another. As my mother used to always say, "If you can't say anything nice, don't say anything at all." Control the anger. Love another.

March 5

"You have heard that it was said, 'You shall not commit adultery.' But I say to you, everyone who looks at a woman with lust has already committed adultery with her in his heart."

MATTHEW 5:27, 28

My daughter was annoyed with me many weekends of her junior and senior high school years. Many times I made her change her outfit before she left the house, and many times I voiced my opinion to her friends about their outfits. Writing across the backside of their shorts draws attention to their rear. Tight shirts draw attention to their breasts. Short skirts, short tops, low tops, no tops. Sounds like Dr. Seuss except there's nothing left for the imagination. Everything is on display.

Jesus extends His Father's commandment about adultery, and we should do our part to keep others from this sin. We must control our actions and our words. We must dress appropriately and teach children to do the same. We have a responsibility that lies unspoken in Jesus' words. Be the example of modesty the world needs. Do not tempt. Cover up.

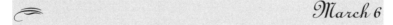

March 6

"Let your 'Yes' mean 'Yes' and your 'No' mean 'No'. Anything more is from the evil one."

MATTHEW 5:37

Most of my youth was filled with days of me saying, "Just kidding." I was constantly joking around. Then I worried that someone might take my jokes seriously. Few did. Most laughed. But as I entered high school, I realized that my "Just kidding" had become a habit. It was actually annoying to me and to others. I could rarely just say what I meant to say. People would look at me and wonder how to take what I was saying. Was I kidding around or was I really lying to get past a situation I had gotten myself into? I had to change.

Jesus knows how to have a good time. He knows when to have fun, and He wants us to be joyful and happy, but He wants us to mean what we say. He does not want us to be "wishy washy" in our answers because He knows that indecision can lead to problems with truth. Too much joking around can lead others astray. He wants us to know the definite answers and to be truthful. Stop all the kidding around. "Yes" and "No."

March 7

"But I say to you, love your enemies, and pray for those who persecute you, that you may be children of your heavenly Father, for he makes his sun rise on the bad and the good, and causes rain to fall on the just and the unjust."

MATTHEW 5:44, 45

I'd love to be a child again. I was fortunate enough to have a childhood packed with simple fun. The worst enemy I can think of in our neighborhood was the boy who shot me in the face with a bb gun packed with concrete. After a couple of days, the redness went away and so did the idea that the boy was the enemy. My parents did not let us hold a grudge for long. They encouraged us to include everyone and hope our friendship would change their meanness.

Jesus calls us to do the hardest things. He wants us to love our enemies and pray for those who persecute us. He wants us to forgive those who hurt us. He wants us to let go of our differences. He tells us that we must be examples of pardoning and of loving and of praying for those who mistreat us. He makes us His children, and as children we cling to Him. As His children, even the most difficult tasks seem possible. As His children, we love and we pray. We forgive.

"Do not store up for yourselves treasures on earth, where moth and decay destroy, and thieves break in and steal. But store up treasures in heaven, where neither moth nor decay destroys, nor thieves break in and steal."

MATTHEW 6:19, 20

J was heartbroken as I pulled my wool blazer from the hall closet and noticed three tiny moth holes on the back. I walked into my living room just in time to see my child, riding on the back rockers of my grandmother's gooseneck chair, fall because the rocker broke. I watched as my child put the straw in a juice box and squirt grape juice on my new playroom carpet. I thought the world would never be the same, and yet the world kept right on moving even though my "treasures" would never be the same.

Jesus tells us that nothing of this earth, man-made, has true value. Little holes, nicks on furniture, dents in cars, or spills on carpet mean absolutely nothing. But how we react to the mishap, how we treat the one who hits our car or spills on our carpet, there's a treasure worth keeping. We are to store treasures in Heaven. People matter. Things don't.

"Do not worry about tomorrow; tomorrow will take care of itself."

MATTHEW 6:34

S eems I worry about the days ahead more than I realize. When my sisters and I ventured down to Florida to bring home some furniture from our parent's condo, I worried about driving the U-Haul fourteen hours back to Nashville. My father had reserved a truck with only two seats, and there were three of us. That gave me a stomach ache. My sister called and changed the reservation. We saw a truck on the highway the day before, and I worried whether I could even drive a vehicle that size. Ours was much smaller. Then, we wondered if everything would fit in the smaller truck. The next day we fit in more than we intended. I was the first to drive and learned quickly how to use the huge mirrors and swing wide. By the time we got to Atlanta to make the first drop, I could back that baby right down the driveway. We made it to Nashville without a hitch. My sister was right as usual. There was nothing to have a stomach ache about. It was all just one big adventure that went better than we could have ever planned.

Jesus tells us not to worry about the tasks in front of us. We are called to handle today because there may be no tomorrow. With all the appointments and events on our calendars, this is more difficult than it seems. We are to try to live in the moment. He will take care of everything if we can just focus on today. No stomach aches, no frets, no concerns, no worries. Live this day.

March 10

"Ask and it will be given to you; seek and you will find; knock and the door will be opened to you. For everyone who asks, receives; and the one who seeks, finds; and to the one who knocks, the door will be opened."

MATTHEW 7:7, 8

For some reason when I think of knocking at a door I'm always picturing Dorothy, the Lion, the Scarecrow, and the Tin Man banging that huge knocker at Emerald City. How intimidating! And not only the door, but then they have to seek the help of that crazy wizard and ask to be taken home. The journey down the yellow brick road is not easy. She asks and receives direction and help only to be told that she has to do more. She seeks and she finds that what she has been looking for has been right at her feet all along. In the end, Dorothy is given all she needs, her final destination, her home. She discovers that what she seeks has always been within her reach and, of course, "there's no place like home."

Jesus knows us well. He knows that we think there are others who need more than we do or that we are not worthy of our requests. He says to us today, do not run away. Ask and I will give you opportunities. Seek and I will show you the way. Knock and I will open the door that will guide you home. He has enough for everyone, and what He has is always within our reach, but there's a road to follow. He wants us to ask. He wants us to bang the huge knocker and tread down the long hallway in search. We will find Him waiting.

"How narrow the gate and constricted the road that leads to life. And those who find it are few."

MATTHEW 7:14

Walking down the narrow stone streets of Toledo, in Spain, my mom and daughters and I enjoyed shopping the many vendors who displayed their goods right on the sidewalks. As we slowly walked another hill and shopped, I noticed a doorway, covered by a leather flap with a cross above the tiny stone opening and a beggar outside. I could not help but pull back the leather flap. To my surprise and delight, there were several short pews in rows with a handful of people kneeling before the exposed Blessed Sacrament. I stepped inside, and as the leather flap dropped behind me, the bustling of the street was silenced. I knelt.

Jesus informs us that His way is not the easy way. He wants us to pull away from where the crowds gather and guide our families down the narrow roads that lead to Him. He promises us life. Through the small opening, there will not be many, but those who find Him, will have it all. Search for the gate. Follow His lead to life.

"Everyone who listens to these words of mine and acts on them will be like a wise man who built his house on rock. The rain fell, the floods came, and the winds blew and buffeted the house. But it did not collapse; it had been set solidly on rock."

MATTHEW 7:24, 25

As a family we go to Florida on vacation almost every year. When I went as a young girl, and as I go now, I am still awed by the talent of some who build sand castles. We all know that they will be gone by the next morning, and yet hours are spent building, oftentimes, very elaborate structures. Those built simply with sand are washed away quickly. Those built with sand and decorated with shells and sticks last a little longer, but soon leave only the decorations in a heap. But castles built with shells as the base and with shells included throughout the entire structure last for days.

Jesus calls us to build a firm foundation for our families. He calls us to work hard to make our homes look nice and our families behave well, to do more. He wants us to build families strong in faith, strong in love for Jesus and for one another. Then we can go from the family and build foundations of faith in our schools and our businesses and our communities. Set solid.

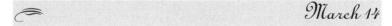

March 13

"But woe to you who are rich, / for you have received your consolation. / But woe to you who are filled now, / for you will be hungry. / Woe to you who laugh now, / for you will grieve and weep."

LUKE 6:24, 25

Television sensationalizes wealth. Reality shows give us the over-the-top view of lives filled with worldly possessions. We see other shows too that reveal how our TV idols live now, and we are saddened by stories of their addictions and their lack of family stability. Not all, but many, we see have used their wealth to destroy themselves. And we know it is not just all on TV.

Jesus certainly does not want us to be in a constant state of hunger and sadness. But He does expect us to share the wealth. He expects us to use whatever good we have in this life to help others to have a good life, too. This life we have been given is meant to be shared, and not just in the sense of dropping money in the poor box. Jesus wants us to make others happy. He wants us to console, to touch, to give. And He wants us to use the means we are given, whether it is just a smile, or an hour of our time, or an ounce of our talent. What we keep for ourselves, may be what destroys us. Give.

March 14

"But to you who hear I say, love your enemies, do good to those who hate you, bless those who curse you, pray for those who mistreat you."

LUKE 6:27, 28

Having a multi-level store oftentimes makes for a theft problem. We try to have a salesperson on each level where there are potential customers, but small areas can get overlooked. It drives me crazy when I get to someone too late who I think has stolen something. I always think of the best things to do or say after they are gone, and it fills my heart with anger and frustration to know they got away with our hard-earned goods. We can only hope and pray that something they take from a Christian store may someday change them.

Jesus wants us to love one another. Period. He wants us to do the hardest tasks for the most difficult people. He knows that we have the capability of compassion and a natural call to help others. He speaks to our hearts to change the world. He wants us to be examples to all of loving those who do us wrong. Regardless of what may have been taken, our time, our pride, or our possessions, Jesus says love, do good, and bless. Pray for those who mistreat.

March 15

"To the person who strikes you on one cheek, offer the other one as well, and from the person who takes your cloak, do not withhold even your tunic."

LUKE 6:29

I once had the painful job of telling a local author that we could not sell his book in our store. He immediately began cursing those who had anything to do with my beliefs, my teachings, and my upbringing. Right in the front of my own store, he gave me an earful and proceeded to threaten to throw me through the front glass window. I was humiliated, tongue tied, and shocked. I had nothing more to say to him but to thank him for his opinion and apologize that things did not work out. I almost made it, but I couldn't leave it alone. A customer asked about it, and I sloughed it off and let it go as a simple disagreement, but I told every employee of his strike against me. I just couldn't keep my mouth shut.

Jesus tells us that He knows what it's like to be ridiculed in front of others. He knows how hard it is, but He wants us to let it go. He tells us that for the love of God, we can do anything. Humiliation, left alone, dies quickly. Humiliation with retaliation festers into an all out infection. We are called to be the bigger person. Let it go.

"Give to everyone who asks of you, and from the one who takes what is yours do not demand it back."

LUKE 6:30

I think most of us give every day without the expectation of getting something in return. We have waited only to be disappointed. We serve our families and our workplaces and our communities only to be asked to give more. I have a friend who is constantly volunteering at the schools her children attend. I know how much work she does and how much time and energy she puts into their causes. I never see her name on any program with the names of the other volunteers. I know she gives credit to everyone but herself.

Jesus tells us that those who give their time and service to others are on the right track. Give to all who ask. When others steal our ideas and our work and our honor, we are told to let it go. When others get the recognition we deserve, we are to let them have the reward on this earth. We do not need acknowledgement for our deeds to continue to serve. Give and then give more.

"Do to others as you would have them do to you."

LUKE 6:31

I love to be romanced. I love to get roses and to be taken out to eat without making the plans. I love to be surprised at the airport by my family after a long journey. I love for my children to run through the back yard hurrying to give me a hug after school. I love for my college kids to call for no reason. I love for others to speak kind about me. I love to make someone smile. I love for friends to visit.

Jesus calls us to think of everything we would love to have done for us and do those things for others. Every day and in every way do as we would like to have done. Send flowers, make plans, surprise someone, hug another, call, write, speak kindly, smile, visit. Whatever it takes, because He knows the return is well worth the effort. Do.

"If you lend money to those from whom you expect repayment, what credit [is] that to you? Even sinners lend to sinners, and get back the same amount."

LUKE 6:34

We have some "regulars" at our bookstore who come to see my husband and me and to buy candles and to tell their stories. They barely have enough to pay their light bill, but they burn their "prayer candles" faithfully. I began giving a man and his wife twice the number of candles they could afford, and when the young man was laid off work, my husband, Allen, paid a couple of his electric bills. I told Allen we would never see that money again, but the man came back several times and paid a few dollars and told a few stories. Then he just stopped coming by the store. "I knew that money was gone," but Allen couldn't have cared less about the money. He wondered what happened in the rest of the story; to the young man, to his wife and her son and their two grandchildren.

Jesus simply tells us not to work for repayment in this world. If that's what we bank on, then in the long run we will be left with nothing. Empty hands and an empty heart. Do everything expecting nothing in return and we will not be disappointed, here or in life eternal. Give without expectations.

"But rather, love your enemies and do good to them, and lend expecting nothing back; then your reward will be great and you will be children of the Most High, for he himself is kind to the ungrateful and the wicked. Be merciful, just as [also] your Father is merciful."

LUKE 6:35, 36

One weekend I set up a large display of books and gifts at a weekend conference, and a teacher in our diocese sold the items while I went to another gift show and ran the bookstore. As I carried in cases of books and almost finished my display, the man running the conference came storming in the door ranting about almost everything I had done. It was all I could do to shake his hand and tell him I'd be glad to do it over again. As the weekend progressed, I went back a couple of times to help, and the young teacher expressed the need to touch each customer and to tell them God bless you or have a wonderful day. She spoke eye to eye with everyone despite the anger and confusion of many who attended the conference. What I saw as misery, she saw as an opportunity. She took time to be kind.

Jesus reminds us again to expect nothing in return. The world is not always a nice place even to those of us who call ourselves Christian. We must persevere through the ungratefulness and the wickedness. Look them in the eyes. Be kind and merciful.

March 20

"Stop judging and you will not be judged. Stop condemning and you will not be condemned. Forgive and you will be forgiven."

LUKE 6:37

When I think of the word "condemned," I remember an old apartment building downtown that had been boarded up and labeled condemned for several years before it was finally torn down. A huge, beautiful, old structure destroyed with a single blast. I passed by the day after the destruction and could not believe the massive piles of stone. The dust had long since settled, and there was nothing left but heaps of rubble.

Jesus tells us to stop tearing one another down. The words we use with our children and our neighbors and our coworkers can destroy a person in a single blast. Sometimes we may not realize the destruction we can cause. These structures we take for granted to be solid humans actually can be people falling apart from the inside out. Don't light the fuse. Refrain from destruction. Construct.

March 21

"Give and gifts will be given to you; a good measure, packed together, shaken down, and overflowing, will be poured into your lap. For the measure with which you measure will in return be measured out to you."

LUKE 6:38

I watched on TV as a guy showed the world that mint Menthos candies dropped down into a two-liter bottle of Diet Coke

57

caused the Coke to foam and to shoot out of the bottle high into the air. He explained that other sodas and other flavored Menthos had been tried but did not have the same explosive effect. Some would foam. Some would even flow over slightly, but none shot high and overflowed like the proper ingredients.

Jesus wants us to do more than just give to one another. He wants us to put together just the right ingredients so that His gifts have an overflowing effect. He wants us to fill our hearts with His love and His teachings so that every day gifts are overflowing through us to others. It doesn't take much for an explosive effect. One good measure can pour out all over the place. Shake things up. Give.

March 22

"No disciple is superior to the teacher; but when fully trained, every disciple will be like his teacher. Why do you notice the splinter in your brother's eye, but do not perceive the wooden beam in your own?"

LUKE 6:40, 41

*R*unning a retail store that has to be open to the public almost every day of the year except Sundays, I feel it is imperative to have someone who can do everything besides just me. I am fortunate to have more than one such person. Having others who can run your business means being allowed to take days off, go on vacation, and spend time with family. Fully trained coworkers make life simpler. Less stressful. The store runs smoothly and customers are satisfied and business is handled.

Jesus wants us to open our eyes, to learn and to lead. He wants us to do His work on earth and He wants us to do it like He would. Filled with wisdom that comes from His teachings, the teachings of the Church, we can lead in the image of our Teacher, with eyes wide open. We need to be fully trained. We need to be His disciples. Imitate His way.

March 23

"How can you say to your brother, 'Brother, let me remove that splinter in your eye,' when you do not even notice the wooden beam in your own eye?

You hypocrite! Remove the wooden beam from your eye first; then you will see clearly to remove the splinter in your brother's eye."

LUKE 6:42

When my daughter Beth was nine years old, she was running her hand along the chain-linked fence of a softball dugout and flicked a tiny splinter of metal into her eye. I called my eye doctor, and he suggested having her blink continually with her face down in a bowl full of water and see if the fleck would come out. I happened to have some water from Lourdes, which I included in the bowl of water I prepared, and I prayed for her, but the proposed remedy failed and we had go to the doctor. Our eye doctor changed the lens on his glasses several times and tried every tool in his office until finally he used a micro fine drill to flick the piece of metal out the same as it flicked in. Rough day for a little girl and her eye doctor and her mama.

Jesus tells us that the tiny little splinter in another's eye is nothing compared to the big beam in our own eye. I know what it takes just to see a splinter and remove it. I hear loud and clear the importance of dealing with my own faults. I can see clearly that I am no better and even when I think I'm close, I need to search for another tool to work on myself. Jesus lets us know that we will have to make a lot of changes before we can see clearly to help others. Use the proper tools. Work tirelessly.

March 24

"A good person out of the store of goodness in his heart produces good, but an evil person out of a store of evil produces evil; for from the fullness of the heart the mouth speaks."

LUKE 6:45

Buying for our retail store, I have to be careful not to go with general trends. There are always books and gifts that produce quantity sales in the general marketplace and "quick sale," "easy money" items are tempting. But my mom has always bought items for the store with the idea of leading others to Christ, not getting ahead in the marketplace. She has handpicked product so there would be multiple levels of affordability, quality for the One we represent and gifts not seen in every chain store across the U.S. She wants to make a difference by our reputation. She wants it to be all about Him.

Jesus tells us that we are known by what we produce and our fruit is a reflection of ourselves, our actions, our words, and our work. We are responsible for how our children and our community develop and respond to this world. Be prosperous in the ways of Christ. Bear good fruit.

March 25

"Why do you call me, 'Lord, Lord,' but not do what I command? I will show you what someone is like who comes to me, listens to my words, and acts on them."

LUKE 6:46, 47

I cannot tell how many times someone has come into our bookstore and asked why we Catholics do something or believe something, and I have to get the answer for them from a book. I admit that I know why I do and believe, but I'd like to give them the official Church teaching for the answer. Thank goodness the *Catechism of the Catholic Church* and many other great reference books have good indexes.

Jesus speaks clearly about knowing the foundations of our faith. He wants us to grow and to know our faith so that we are not just followers but leaders. We are given opportunities every day and He wants us to do more than just listen and believe. He wants us to know and act with truth. We are called to help others find the Answer. Come to Him. Listen and act.

March 26

"That one is like a person building a house, who dug deeply and laid the foundation on rock; when the flood came, the river burst against that house but could not shake it because it had been well built. But the one who listens and does not act is like a person who built a house on the ground without a foundation. When the river burst against it, it collapsed at once and was completely destroyed."

LUKE 6:48, 49

*M*y junior year of high school, I approached one of the Dominican sisters who taught me and told her point-blank that I was beginning to question my Catholic faith. I thought she may jump on some tirade, but much to my surprise she responded calmly by saying, "You know, it's good to question your faith because when you search for the truth, it will only make you stronger in your beliefs," or something like that. Her trust and belief in my foundation strongly influenced my journey.

Jesus speaks to us in terms we use daily. We are in charge of laying firm foundations. He is not speaking of what was done for us, He is speaking of what we are to do. We cannot be complacent in our beliefs. We must learn truth so we are strong enough to go out and teach and be an example. A foundation built on truth will save us from being wiped out in the daily turbulence. Be solid.

March 27

"And then they will see the Son of Man coming in a cloud with power and great glory. But when these signs begin to happen, stand erect and raise your heads because your redemption is at hand."

LUKE 21:27, 28

One Spring my mom and I made the long trip to Yugoslavia to visit the place where hundreds of thousands of pilgrims believe Our Blessed Mother appeared to five children in Medjugorje. I will never forget standing in the field next to the church waiting for my mom as she went to confession. Suddenly, someone called out "look at the sun." Every head in that field looked toward the sky and whether kneeling or sitting, everybody stood. Every action stopped. Every person hoped for a sign, longed to see the sun pulsate or spin; longed to confirm that Mary's presence was real. There were a few people who were pointing and talking to one another. Then suddenly, as quickly as it had all began, it stopped, and we went back to what we were doing.

Jesus wants us to be aware of the signs He sends. He speaks today of the end times and our redemption. If we are paying attention, if we are aware of all He is sending, we will be saved. We must not get so caught up in the ways of this world that we miss our chance to be saved. He wants us to pay attention. Watch.

"Do not weep…. Young man, I tell you, arise!"

LUKE 7:13, 14

e all know parents who have dealt with the loss of a child. Young or old, sick or well, to lose a child is the most unbearable moment I can fathom. My parents have buried a son days old, a pre-teen grandson, a nephew in his teens, a son in his thirties, a son-in-law in his thirties, and a brother in his fifties. Their faith sees them through because they must hear Jesus say, "Do not weep — these young men will rise." Hope in the resurrection is all we have to hold on to during these times.

Jesus tells us that He can identify with us because His mother too would lose her only Son. He knew the pain Mary would go through and the pain we go through, and He chose to die so that all could have eternal life. He says to us, "do not weep." This pain is temporary. These children will rise. Our hope is in the Resurrection. Our reward is eternal life.

"Go and tell John what you have seen and heard: the blind regain their sight, the lame walk, lepers are cleansed, the deaf hear, the dead are raised, the poor have the good news proclaimed to them. And blessed is the one who takes no offense at me."

LUKE 7:22, 23

n old high school friend of mine moved back into town and decided it was her mission to help organize our family bookstore and help my mother with displays. She built shelves and bought Tupperware and helped my mother in the wee hours of the morning. I was grateful and yet jealous of her ideas and her hard work. I joked and criticized instead of enjoying the relief. I constantly wondered, "what I would come in to" as I entered the store each day. She was a great relief for my mother. She brought new, fresh ideas and energy.

Jesus speaks to all of us who would prefer to do everything our own way. He encourages us to be like John, who had given his life to do what God wanted; to baptize and to bring people to the faith.

Then Jesus arrives and can do things with great proof and instead of taking offense to His ease of turning souls, John is relieved. Jesus wants us to graciously accept the help He sends. No offense.

"To what shall I compare this generation? It is like children who sit in marketplaces and call to one another, 'We played the flute for you, but you did not dance, we sang a dirge but you did not mourn.'"

MATTHEW 11:16, 17

*O*urs is a generation of instant gratification. When I do anything, I like to know immediately if it works or if someone likes it. I write Saint biographies for a holy card company. When I regularly send new ones off to be printed, they are not gone more than a few weeks and I wonder where the product is and why they're not in stores yet. Hello. What takes so long?

Jesus calls us to relax and enjoy the music. He wants us to stop worrying about the results and enjoy the journey, especially with one another. If we are always looking for the instant reward, we miss the sheer joy of the work. Enjoy the children. Enjoy the song. Enjoy the journey. Our reward is out there. Relax.

"What did you go out to the desert to see — a reed swayed by the wind? Then what did you go out to see? Someone dressed in fine garments? Those who dress luxuriously and live sumptuously are found in royal palaces."

LUKE 7:24, 25

I had great expectations when I traveled to Fátima to see where Mary had appeared to three children on a hillside. I envisioned a slight hill, dirt, and a small grotto in the place where Mary once stood. I saw a massive concrete lot with churches at each end and a tree with fencing around it on the side of a chapel. I had to search for the message I had come to receive. And, once again, my message came through the people of faith who visited with no expectations.

Jesus puts people and places in our lives for a reason. There is nothing that happens by chance. Oftentimes we do not get what we expect, and we are disappointed. Jesus teaches us to seek the message that is intended not the one we expect. Nothing is by chance.

April 1

"'Behold, I am sending my messenger ahead of you, / he will prepare your way before you.' / I tell you, among those born of women, no one is greater than John; yet the least in the kingdom of God is greater than he."
LUKE 7:27, 28

*N*eedless to say, messengers often get the raw end of the deal. I guess that's why the saying is "Don't shoot the messenger." The "message" is just not what people care to hear. Our children do not want to hear that they need to be good examples to their siblings and others. They do not care to hear another word about responsibility and love for one another and kindness. Or for all that matter, to clean their room, brush their teeth, and comb their hair. But truthfully, parents as well as managers and teachers and other professionals are simply messengers. We're here to offer the way to a better, more successful life. Give us a break.

Jesus speaks to us of a messenger sent ahead to prepare the way. And He continues to send us great examples and leaders of the Church such as St. Catherine of Siena, St. Thomas Aquinas, and St. Teresa of Ávila. We hear about women who have fought for social justice such as Dorothy Day. Countless messengers such St. Thérèse of Lisieux, St. Dominic, St. Francis, Mother Teresa, Edith Stein, Maria Goretti, and Gianna Beretta Molla who have dedicated their lives to spreading the Gospel. We are told to follow and, in turn, by example, we too can be a messenger of the "way." Our path is prepared. Lead on.

April 2

"For John the Baptist came neither eating food nor drinking wine, and you said, 'He is possessed by a demon.' The Son of Man came eating and drinking and you said, 'Look, he is a glutton and a drunkard, a friend of tax collectors and sinners.'"

LUKE 7:33, 34

I once had an employee who found fault with everyone to make herself look good and feel good. By the end of each week she'd tried to convince me and herself that she was far superior to the others. The girl who worked on the same floor never caught a break. If she talked to customers for any length of time, she neglected tasks. If she did tasks, she neglected customers. She was on the phone too long, she didn't finish writing orders, was too loud or too quiet. She didn't fill out forms completely or she was too meticulous. There was no way she could win, and unfortunately I took the bait until my employee started on her next victim. Then I discovered that insecurity and poor work ethics were this employee's own problems and not those with whom she worked.

Jesus points out that the world is never quite satisfied with the messenger. We are so busy finding fault in others to make ourselves look better that we miss the message. We must work with one another and accept one another and ourselves as we are; as one body. No comparing. Focus on the message.

April 3

"But wisdom is vindicated by all her children."

LUKE 7:35

*F*irst and foremost I would like to note that wisdom is a woman who is defended by her children. We have all heard plenty of wise cracks about wise men versus wise women. I have read all kinds of funny quips about three wise women arriving at the manger and not just bringing great gifts, but immediately cleaning the place, changing the baby, attending to the mom, telling the father what he should be doing, and making dinner. I know that as a Christian my choices are scrutinized, so they had better be wise. I also know that my children have my back. To them I am one wise chick and they need not know any differently.

All joking aside, Jesus gives us the gift of wisdom through the power of the Holy Spirit. Used to their full potential, the gifts of the Spirit nourish us to lead the kind of life that God meant for us; a life that is focused on our return to Him. In our wisdom we make the choices that bring others and ourselves to the living Christ. Be wise.

"I give praise to you, Father, Lord of heaven and earth, for although you have hidden these things from the wise and the learned you have revealed them to the childlike."

MATTHEW 11:25

I have a gentleman who comes into our bookstore on occasion, and if I see him, he always has some amazing story about how God works in his life. He has received incredible signs that his work, which he believes is to read and to tell about the lives of the Saints, the visions of Mary, and the teachings of Christ, is approved from above. He's constantly reminding me that he is like a kid who just wants more, and the more he gets the more he wants others to have also. He tells everybody about the wonders of our God no matter what they think or say or how they react. He is always excited about some gift he's received.

Jesus tells us to listen to the children. Their innocent comments are often close to God. It's like they have spoken to Him recently and can remember the simplicity of His message before the world junks it all up. Nothing God has to say is difficult to understand. May we be open to Him like a kid who just wants more because every day He has so much more to reveal to us. Stay simple.

"Come to me, all you who labor and are burdened, and I will give you rest. Take my yoke upon you and learn from me, for I am meek and humble of heart; and you will find rest for yourselves."

MATTHEW 11:28, 29

*M*y sister has always juggled more than one event or job each day for years. I would joke with her when a spot on her kitchen calendar had an open space, and she would respond that she just hadn't filled in a volleyball tournament or scout meeting or tutoring session. She teaches grade school math and science during the day, college algebra or statistics at night, sometimes coaches or tutors in between, runs to sporting or social events of her own children, edits textbooks online, and always manages a traditional southern Sunday supper. And all of this is merely the base of her week. However, she believes in everything she does and although she could let go of something, she wouldn't, because what would she choose? Well, maybe the supper.

Jesus speaks to us as our Comforter. He knows we tire of constantly serving others, showing compassion, being the "one" everyone can rely on, being the "bottom line," the parent, the chairperson, the leader, and the one who loves unconditionally. He has been there. He is there and He tells us to believe in everything we do, learn from Him, and rest in Him. All things done in His name are made easier by Him. He is meek and humble of heart. Find rest.

"Do you see this woman? When I entered your house, you did not give me water for my feet, but she has bathed them with her tears and wiped them with her hair. You did not give me a kiss, but she has not ceased kissing my feet since the time I entered. You did not anoint my head with oil, but she anointed my feet with ointment."

LUKE 7:44–46

When I'm at home, I love being at home. I like to spend time with my children and have time to straighten the house and cook a proper meal, put away the laundry and make lunches. And, like other parents, I realize that most of what I do is unappreciated. When I'm at work, I love to be at work. I love buying just the right merchandise with certain customers in mind. I enjoy suggesting great books or gifts whether for enjoyment or for specific needs, sharing faith stories, laughing and crying and working with financials and inventory (I like numbers). I have to say, some works are noticed and some done unseen.

Jesus says that all our work, no matter how minor we think it is, done with love and sincerity will not go unnoticed by God. When we are working at the feet of Jesus, He acknowledges all we do. And what more could we need this day than to be acknowledged and appreciated by Jesus? Work with love.

"So I tell you, her many sins have been forgiven; hence, she has shown great love. But the one to whom little is forgiven, loves little."

LUKE 7:47

When I was young, I would play with my sister's goldfish she had won at the state fair. One day, the little guy wiggled through my fingers onto the floor and, before I could grab him, squirmed down the vent in the floor. I rushed to the kitchen, grabbed a knife and pried open the vent to retrieve the dust-filled mess. I cleaned his little gills and dropped him into his bowl. The fish died three days later. For weeks my sister gave me the silent treatment. She would not speak to me, she would not invite me anywhere, and she would not let me use anything of hers. It was rough. I asked her forgiveness daily and when she finally forgot or forgave, I'm not sure which, I was happy beyond words.

Jesus explains today that forgiveness perpetuates love. He wants us to be examples of forgiveness and to teach forgiveness so that all can live in love and happiness and peace. As this woman, we are asked to show great love, to forgive, and to go out and perpetuate love so that others will do the same. Forgive and be happy. Live in love.

"Every kingdom divided against itself will be laid to waste, and no town or house divided against itself will stand."

MATTHEW 12:25

One of the smartest things I've watched a coach do whose team had no chance of winning was to get the opponents working against themselves. The coach had the players frustrate the most aggressive player by double-teaming him. When his teammates shut him out of the game, he was angry. There was yelling back and forth among them, then players were benched and the team began to slowly beat themselves. The coach picked on player after player until he divided the entire team. His guys were able to play their own game well and ended up the winners. Pretty good strategy for a lower ranked team.

Jesus says the only way we will make it in the world is if we stand together. We see our own churches go through tough times when a new pastor arrives or a group disagrees with decisions. Jesus warns us against division. We must stay together. We are called to outsmart evil, to stand against the harshness, and to gather for the sake of the Kingdom. We are challenged to plan our strategy. Take the win.

April 9

"Either declare the tree good and its fruit is good, or declare the tree rotten and its fruit is rotten, for a tree is known by its fruit."

MATTHEW 12:33

Many times in a given week I am identified as one of my children's mother. I can usually tell by the tone of their statement whether to admit to the accusation or not. "Oh, you're Julia's mom!" or "You're Sarah's mom?" or "Wait, you're Will's mom." My first thought is usually, "Why, what have they done?" but the realization is that we are known by these fruits. The hope is that all the talk about good manners and kindness has been heard and put to use. If so, we will never have to wonder whether or not we should admit our parenthood.

Jesus tells us that we are known for what we produce. Whether we accomplish a task in our community or at work, or cause a problem at school, or make others aware of a harmful movie, or serve at church, we become known as, "Oh, you're the one who...." Jesus wants us to be good and to do good so that what or who we are associated with will go and do the same. Produce good fruit.

April 10

"By your words you will be acquitted, and by your words you will be condemned."

MATTHEW 12:37

My mother used many sayings about kind words while we were growing up because she knew how words could hurt or heal. "If you can't say something nice, don't say anything at all" (thank you, Thumper). "Keep your words soft and sweet, just in case you have to eat them." "You catch more flies with honey than with vinegar." We weren't fond of eating dirt and filth any more than we were fond of getting our mouths washed out with soap. Best for us to keep all that came from our mouths clean.

Jesus speaks to us about our use of words. We can make or break another's day by what we say. We have actually seen where a mother's words have caused a young girl to take her life. Words can destroy, but they can also heal. They can make people laugh, and they can bring people to love. We are told to choose our words carefully because the very life we save may be our own eternal life. Speak kind words.

April 11

"My mother and my brothers are those who hear the word of God and act on it."

LUKE 8:21

One Saturday in our bookstore, I had a seven year old boy ask me if I wanted him to pray for me. "Of course, I would love for you to pray for me." I thought he meant in general, but he meant immediately. He reached out, and I knelt on one knee as he laid his hand on my head. Out loud, in the middle of the holy card section of the store, this young man began, "May the Lord keep watch between you and me when we are out of each other's sight. If you mistreat my daughters, or take other wives besides my daughters, remember that even though no one else is about, God will be witness between you and me. Amen." I responded, "Amen." At that point, I felt we were bonded in the family of God, he as my brother. He smiled and said, "I learned that at Church."

Jesus speaks to us about His family. We all want to be a part of the family of God and He welcomes us. He says simply, "Hear the Word and act." As sisters and as brothers to one another, be open and act. Immediately.

April 12

"And some seed fell on rich soil and produced fruit. It came up and grew and yielded thirty, sixty, and a hundredfold." "Whoever has ears to hear ought to hear."

MARK 4:8, 9

J took some time in the fall to work in the gardens around our house. I had left them to themselves for years, and they were dry and ragged looking. I pulled out all the dead bushes that had long ago sucked the nutrients from the soil. I took the natural dirt and mixed it with new, rich soil and watered down the new soil with bottles of blue colored "minerals." I tended and I planted, and for weeks my hands and forearms ached. As spring arrived, I noticed my efforts were not in vain.

Jesus shares with us the importance of rich soil. He tells us that anyone can hear His word. It is available to everyone in every different language. But He tells us today to take His word and tend to it and take care every day to make it grow in the hearts of all who will hear. We are to spread His word and help it to produce good fruit and multiply. Our efforts will not be in vain. Work the soil.

April 13

"To anyone who has, more will be given and he will grow rich; from anyone who has not, even what he has will be taken away. This is why I speak to them in parables, because 'they look but do not see and hear but do not listen or understand.'"

MATTHEW 13:12, 13

A ny parent knows that the best way to get through to our children is to keep at it. Keep telling the stories and making the rules and talking, because they listen but they do not understand. Yet, they just agree so that we will be quiet, but we must continue with words and examples. Some time from now, something they have seen or heard will rise to the top of their memory and make a difference. I know the back of my consciousness has brought forth lessons from my childhood that have helped me to choose between right and wrong many times in my life. Somewhere back there a small voice has saved me from a huge mistake.

Jesus explains to us that He speaks in parables for our own benefit. Every person listens to the stories with their own expectations, and so the interpretations benefit us in different ways. But the stories are easy to remember, and as life goes on they help us on our journey in ways we may not even realize. They may make a difference even after we are gone. Continue to tell the stories.

"The mystery of the kingdom of God has been granted to you. But to those outside everything comes in parables, so that / 'they may look and see but not perceive, / and hear and listen but not understand, / in order that they may not be converted and be forgiven.'"

MARK 4:11, 12

$\mathcal{A}$good mystery keeps us in suspense until the very end. When we were young, Nancy Drew and the Hardy Boys were the big mystery solvers, and my brothers and sister seemed to read them all the time. These young detectives would gather clues as to the answer and oftentimes make us think we could figure the whole thing out until in the end when we'd be totally surprised. Good detectives follow all the twists and turns and subplots and do solve the mystery for us all. But we remain in suspense until the answer is revealed.

Jesus tells us that the mystery of the kingdom has been given us. We are on the inside track. We hear what He is telling us and we understand the message. Jesus wants us to follow all the twists and turns and pass on the answers as we pray and we listen and are forgiven. We are the lucky ones to whom His message is revealed. We remain close until the answer comes again in glory. Revel in the mystery.

"The seed is the word of God."

LUKE 8:11

$\mathcal{S}$omewhere around preschool to first grade, each of my children brought home paper cups with small plants beginning to peek through the soil. Some were very careful to care for their new beginnings, and others were completely forgetful. We had plants die in a couple of weeks, live for months, and live to have the roots shooting through the bottom of the cup in need of transplanting. I'm no green thumb, but I am pretty sure the plants should have at least been watered and put into larger pots.

Jesus tells us that His word is merely a seed. It will surely die if we do not take care to nourish and to tend and to help it grow. We are responsible for its development. We are needed to spread it into places that will allow it to multiply. The word of God is only the beginning as it peeks through in our lives. Nourish His word.

"No one who lights a lamp conceals it with a vessel or sets it under a bed; rather, he places it on a lampstand so that those who enter may see the light. For there is nothing hidden that will not become visible, and nothing secret that will not be known and come to light."

LUKE 8:16, 17

*P*roper lighting makes a big difference. Our front porch has never been very inviting. The railing up the stairs was half rusted and the bushes were overgrown and most of the stepping stones to get to the porch were cracked. Consequently, I never minded the tiny, dim porch lamps that screamed "Please use the back door." During the fall season, we had a new walkway poured, put in all new bushes, took off the hand railing, replaced the rotted ceiling with siding, and put in large, new lanterns that lure visitors to use the front entrance. Set back off the highway, our home now says, "All are welcome."

Jesus tells us that He was not born a man to be kept a secret. He did not preach and teach messages that we are to hide within ourselves. His light, His life, His death, and His resurrection are meant to make a difference to us all. We are asked to light our big lanterns so that we invite all into our hearts and our homes and spread the good news. Make visible the message. Shine brightly.

"Take care what you hear. The measure with which you measure will be measured out to you, and still more will be given to you. To the one who has, more will be given; from the one who has not, even what he has will be taken away."

MARK 4:24, 25

*W*e are infiltrated with information daily. We hear from people in conversations, on the Internet, on the television, and on our phones. We've become a keyboard people. We cut, copy, and paste. We type and we text, and it is often difficult to determine which stories are true or false. Someone entrusts a secret to someone else, and before we realize what has happened, we're hearing about our family on another child's Facebook. The new age of technology has heightened our awareness of "who we can trust."

Jesus warns us to take care of words we are given. People in our society need others whom they can truly trust, who will not only care about what they're told but who can keep their words safe. We need to take time with one another; to have the old fashioned cup of coffee at the kitchen table and share words. Talk with others. Treasure what you hear.

April 18

"But blessed are your eyes, because they see, and your ears, because they hear. Amen, I say to you, many prophets and righteous people longed to see what you see but did not see it, and to hear what you hear but did not hear it."

MATTHEW 13:16, 17

We are fortunate to live during times when witnesses to the love of Jesus Christ are set before us. Sure the media often finds something to kill a great Christian moment, but that is just evil trying to down play good. The works of Bl. Pope John Paul II and Bl. Mother Teresa of Calcutta are acknowledged in mounds of books and hundreds of Internet pages. We hear and see wonderful stories on television and Youtube of people going out on missions to other countries that need assistance in the medical field and in teaching and caring and love.

Jesus calls us to open our eyes and our ears to the witnesses He has put in our lives. They could be a local priest or minister, a sister, a client, a coworker, a teacher, a friend, or a woman on the street. Jesus tells us we are fortunate because we live after His resurrection and are capable of making sense out of all He sends us. But we must live open to the gifts. We must read and listen and learn. He will bless us.

April 19

"Of its own accord the land yields fruit, first the blade, then the ear, then the full grain in the ear. And when the grain is ripe, he wields the sickle at once, for the harvest has come."

MARK 4:28, 29

There is nothing like a fresh, homegrown tomato. I can remember my mom buying fresh tomatoes and putting the ones that still had a little green on top in the window sill to ripen. Once they turned just the right shade of red, she'd cut them to put with our green beans or on our bacon, lettuce, and tomato sandwiches. The rich, fresh flavor of a ripe, red tomato just cannot be beat.

Jesus tells us again about the importance of planting the word of God deep inside ourselves. He's told us many stories about what we have to do to make that word grow and become ripe. Today He says we must continue to weed and feed ourselves so that like a fresh, home grown tomato, we're ripe at the time of harvest. We don't want to be put in the window sill and made to wait. We don't want the outside world with its sprays and preservatives to alter our freshness. Grow the word. Keep it fresh. Be ready at the time the sickle wields. Harvest well.

April 20

"Let them grow together until harvest; then at harvest time I will say to the harvesters, 'First collect the weeds and tie them in bundles for burning; but gather the wheat into my barn.'"

MATTHEW 13:30

We see our children in groups with other children at school or in the neighborhood. We have them come home with words and actions and facial expressions we know they have learned from others. We wish there was a giant bubble we could keep them in to protect them from the outside world, but truth be told, the choices they make around their peers can make them stronger. They can be well grounded and be a positive influence or turn like weeds and wither and fall.

Jesus gives us the visual image of the field loaded with weeds among wheat. Now I know how difficult it is not to accidentally pull up some flowers when I'm weeding the garden. Suddenly I realize how important it is not to spend my life too close to the weeds. I know we are to be examples to one another, but we also must be careful not to be swayed even slightly by the ways of this world. We do not want ourselves or anyone we love to be pulled with the weed bundles. Surround yourselves and your family and your friends with all that is good. Strengthen one another. Grow together in faith.

"The kingdom of heaven is like a treasure buried in a field, which a person finds and hides again, and out of joy goes and sells all that he has and buys that field."

MATTHEW 13:44

When we were young, my best friend and I found the area where our school dumped all their old desks until they had enough, I'm guessing, to burn. They were stashed at the end of a huge field attached to school property and were piled in a ditch. We gathered the ones we wanted and made an area for a club. Each day before we left, we covered our new area the best we could so others would not take what we had worked on. We arrived one afternoon in time to see a neighborhood boy carrying off one of our desks. We warned him never to return or to tell anyone else as if the field now belonged to us.

Jesus explains that if we know what awaits those who follow Him, we will let go of everything to try to obtain it. We are called to gather all that we have and use it to seek what gains us heaven. We are challenged to arrive early and warn others. He tells us to sell it all, trust His words, and hold on to the One who can save us. Pull up a desk, let go of everything, and listen to and learn from the stories. They tell of the Kingdom.

"Again, the kingdom of heaven is like a net thrown into the sea, which collects fish of every kind. When it is full they haul it ashore and sit down to put what is good into buckets. What is bad they throw away."

MATTHEW 13:47, 48

I've always loved to walk the beach with my children and look for shells. Where we vacation in Florida, the sand is covered with shells and the mass quantity allows a regular seeker to be choosey. My girls however always seem to choose the ugliest shells; the ones with odd bumps all over or the broken ones. They know that underneath, there lies beauty. They know that it's not all about the outside appearance. They see the possibilities.

Jesus tells us today that He will be choosey when it comes to awarding the kingdom. He wants us to strive to be the best we can be; to be holy as has been His example. We all have ugliness of some sort, but He knows that underneath, there lies beauty. He wants us to recognize our imperfections and our brokenness and pray for God to heal our worse parts. He challenges us to be gathered in with the haul. He wants us to "make the cut." We are to work to be chosen because we are all possibilities. Be beautiful.

"Then every scribe who has been instructed in the kingdom of heaven is like the head of a household who brings from his storeroom both the new and the old."

MATTHEW 13:52

My husband and I have played with restoring old cars since we've been married. We have never really had the time to finish many projects ourselves, but we have had fun trying. The most important idea I have learned about restoration is that the cars worth anything are the ones put back with as many of the old, original parts as possible. Old cars are deemed more valuable, the more authentic their parts. We have always had to mix some newly fabricated parts with the old parts, but the old parts are necessary.

Jesus talks to us about the importance of preserving parts of the old laws with the new to make it to the kingdom. He speaks to us directly as leaders to teach our children and our communities the importance of traditional teachings. He tells us that He knows the world we live in. He knows we look for new ways in our modern world, but to be authentic, to be deemed valuable enough to make it to the Kingdom, we must keep the old with the new. Preserve what God intended.

"Why are you terrified, O you of little faith?"

MATTHEW 8:26

Managing a family business with my husband means a one-job shot at income. I worry about everything from the back office to the selling floor. In good times, I worry about how much to give away and how much to use for maintenance and upkeep. In hard times, I worry about keeping employees, friends, and families, spending on new product and overhead costs. I work constantly with numbers because we don't want to just stay afloat; we want to lead others to the shore.

Jesus understands the storms in our lives. He knows that this world is unsure, and in our fear we turn to other worldly help. But He tells us today to have faith. He hears our cries in the midst of the storm, and He will not let us be swallowed up by the world. He calls us to be strong people of faith. In the midst of the worst storms, He calms. In our greatest fears, He comforts. We are called and encouraged to put all we have, all we do, in His hands. Have faith.

<hr>

April 25

"Go home to your family and announce to them all that the Lord in his pity has done for you.'"

MARK 5:19

One year a friend of mine was having medical issues, and I spent a lot of time attending to her needs. It made me feel good to help her even though she had her own family she could call upon. Months went by, and I got a little spiritual direction to actually disconnect myself from the idea that someone could not survive without me. Although the deeds made me feel good, I was hurting my family. My daughters informed me that they actually resented the time I had spent away from them; like they were my second choice. I had no idea.

Jesus speaks clearly when He tells us today to go home to our family. This is where we are to begin. Our work is plentiful right under our own roof and in our own communities. We cannot possibly fix the entire world. We can be Christlike, we can love, we can reach out. We need to be examples, and we should help others, but we also must take care of the people directly in front of us first. Go home to your family. Allow no resentfulness.

<hr>

April 26

"Daughter, your faith has saved you. Go in peace and be cured of your affliction."

MARK 5:34

I stood pressed against the metal gate waiting for the arrival of Bl. Pope John Paul II. The huge crowd roared as he started

78

around St. Peter's square in his open cart, stopping to shake hands and impart blessings. I thought if I could just touch him I'd be satisfied for life. As he approached, an Italian woman was screaming for me to hold up her child for the Pope to bless. I knew it meant no chance for me, but in this one hectic moment I got it all. He stopped to bless the child and shake my hand, and I took his picture at point blank range. The touch of his hand I'll never forget. The peace in my heart was enough for a lifetime.

Today Jesus offers us that one small touch that can bring us peace. He calls us to have complete faith in Him. Once again He cures a woman because of her belief. One small touch. One huge moment. Enough for a lifetime.

April 27

"'Do not weep any longer, for she is not dead, but sleeping.... Child, arise!'"
LUKE 8:52, 54

My father lay in the hospital on every machine imaginable to keep him alive. A nurse came out to the waiting area and told us to call the priest and his brother and tell them it was time for him to die. Not ten minutes after I had made the calls, his doctor came out to say it was not time for him to die but he did give us a scare. Today my dad is healthy and well, thanks to God's hand, many prayers, and his doctor's persistence.

Jesus talks to us about sorrow. He point blank does not like us to be sad. He explains to us that death is a time of temporary separation just as when we sleep. But He knows that we will rejoin one another someday. Jesus knows how difficult the loss of a loved one is because He knows how hard it will be for His mother. He has great care and compassion for sadness. He comforts us with the promise of the Resurrection. Feel the touch of His hands. Trust in His promise. Do not weep. There is so much more.

April 28

"Do you believe that I can do this?"
MATTHEW 9:28

I had never seen the likes of true believers before I stood, more than once, and watched nurses and family and friends push wheelchairs down the hill from the hospital at Lourdes in France to bathe the sick in the miraculous waters. Day after day they persistently believe in the possibility of being cured. Long lines, bad weather, and cranky tourists do not distract from the expectation. The volunteers and families and patients are focused on the next cure because they truly believe.

Jesus asks us a question and waits for our response. Anything in the world that we have on our plate, do we believe whole-heartedly that Jesus can take care of it? We can turn the question back to Him, and we hear day after day a persistent, "I made you and I love you and I believe you can." If we love Him and believe, we must turn to Him always. We must not let the lines and the weather and the cranky people around distract us from the expectation of what God can do for those who love Him, who believe. Focus on the next cure.

April 29

"See that no one knows about this."

MATTHEW 9:30

Many times in our parenting lives my husband and I have asked individual children not to let the others know about something we have done for them, not because we play favorites, but because the others knowing would cause difficulty. My daughter Margaret oftentimes spends the night with friends when we go out to dinner as a family. If she hears where we are going it confuses her decision to go with her friend. If my daughter Sarah comes home from college and my daughter Beth has already committed to plans and cannot come home, Beth finds it difficult not to change her plans and throw off the entire group. It is best just to keep certain information between ourselves.

Jesus tells us today that there are times when happenings, coincidences, and miracles are better kept between Him and us. He has certain moments with us that can cause a disturbance with others if they were to hear. Some may think we are a little overboard and others may wonder why they never seem to have the same experiences. He does not have favorites, but some things are just best left kept inside. Keep it inside. Keep it between you and Jesus. His request.

"A prophet is not without honor except in his native place and among his own kin and in his own house."

MARK 6:4

After the publishing of *Bless My Child*, my prayer book for mothers, a girl who I knew quite well jokingly said, "I didn't know you wrote. Heck, I didn't even know you prayed." We both laughed. This is not an unfamiliar response from those who know me. I love to joke around and have fun. Still, I demand a certain amount of respect from my children so they will in turn have respect for others. I like our bookstore to run the way I believe my mother would, something for everyone, and yet all to bring others closer to God. In my little world, people often cannot decide whether or not to take me seriously.

Jesus tells us that we have no place of honor among those who know us best. They grew up with us, they know who we are, and they find our words hard to believe. But this never stopped Him or His apostles, and it can't stop us. Sometimes those around us take in all we say and they just don't let us know. We just have to keep Jesus first, speak the truth, and hope all else falls into place. In our homes and our communities are our toughest tests. Live with honor.

"The harvest is abundant but the laborers are few; so ask the master to send out laborers for this harvest."

MATTHEW 9:37, 38

Asking others to help can oftentimes be more difficult than simply pushing through a task alone. Several years after my mom bought St. Mary's Bookstore, I worked many hours trying to get stock checked in, help on the selling floor, and handle special orders. What I didn't finish at the store, I would take home. Every task was done, but nothing was done well. In retrospect, I was a part-time wife, part-time mother, and a part-time employee, even though I put in full-time hours at each job. After several years, we hired workers to do jobs as they were intended to be done; completely. Not only did my family, my life, and the store run more efficiently, but others were included in the tasks God wanted done.

Jesus calls us today not only to realize that there is so much more work to be done, but also to allow others to join in His work. He knows what we are capable of doing. He understands that oftentimes it's easier if we do it all ourselves, but He wants us to include others and get the job done so we can serve over and over and over. Much more to do.

"Without cost you have received; without cost you are to give."

MATTHEW 10:8

More often than I care to admit, I find myself screeching to my children that they are to do what I asked because I've asked them. I provide food and a home and clothes and the least they can do is help out with the chores around the house. I don't charge them room and board, so I refuse to pay them for their services. Children need to learn that there are certain things in this life they do because they are the right thing to do or because it's nice or because it's a part of being given life. My children learn early that they help out not because of service hours or allowance, but because they are a part of a family or a community that gladly gives to them without cost.

Jesus tells us that He expects us to be of service to one another. He gave life freely. He expects us to give back without cost. The elderly, the poor, the underprivileged, the lonely, the sad, and the lost need our help. Our churches, our schools, and our families need our help. Care for one another without cost. Give freely.

"When they hand you over, do not worry about how you are to speak of what you are to say. You will be given at that moment what you are to say. For it will not be you who speak but the spirit of your Father speaking through you."

MATTHEW 10:19, 20

$\mathcal{M}$y mother taught me years ago, before I give a talk, to ask the Holy Spirit to guide my words. Yet, I can't seem to let go of trying to prepare something to say. I have tried both sheets of paper and note cards in various sizes and colors. The best luck I have had with props so far is a journal with actual readings I just had to deliver. Yet, even after practicing, those were delivered rough and unsteady. All of these gizmos get me through the first 10 minutes of talking then I tend to loosen up. I can feel the Spirit working when I stop with my earthly aids, and I become myself. Words flow and people laugh and ideas and stories are shared by others. It seems the Spirit allows me to get through what I need to do, then He can begin His work and His message.

Jesus tells us not to worry about the words. If we are with Him, the Spirit speaks through us. At this moment, He will give the words. He has sent the Spirit to take care of us in our time of need. He has got our back. We can have confidence in our words as we speak in His name, as we defend the Church, and as He guides us through our day. No worry.

May 4

"No disciple is above his teacher, no slave above his master. It is enough for the disciple that he become like his teacher, for the slave that he become like his master."

MATTHEW 10:24, 25

$\mathcal{M}$y mom has an incredible talent for building displays at our bookstore that really sell the merchandise. She has gladly passed on her talent to anyone and everyone who will listen. The keys are: 1. Everything displayed in odd numbers; 2. Make it big; and 3. Make sure the display tells a story. Everyone who follows those simple rules has created displays that sell. But there are many of us who have strived to do better and those displays have failed time and time again. Oversized and bulky do not draw a customer in and share a story. Small and balanced do not catch a person's attention. I constantly call my mom and tell her the store screams for her help. As she talks me through some ideas I hear a huge sigh of relief throughout the building.

Jesus calls us to be like those He has sent to lead us. Working to be better than the Master does not draw anyone into the story. It may make us feel big for the moment, but it really does not grab anyone's attention. In fact, it could leave us feeling awkward and out of place. Follow the simple rules. Those He has sent to teach us, the examples from His life, give us help and bring relief. Follow the Master.

"Are not two sparrows sold for a small coin? Yet not one of them falls to the ground without your Father's knowledge. Even all the hairs of your head are counted. So do not be afraid; you are worth more than many sparrows."

MATTHEW 10:29, 30

When I was young, my best friend Maureen and I could practically finish each other's sentences. I knew her likes and dislikes and she knew mine. I knew how far to push my own parents as well as her parents. We both knew the neighborhood like the backs of our hands. We spent many hours every day together and naturally came to know more about each other than we knew about our own siblings. Going into second grade our parents let us buy matching blue suede shoes to go with our grey uniforms. We walked to and from school every day together. All summer we swam together and bowled in the same bowling league. We were inseparable, and our friendship was worth more to me than anything I possessed.

Jesus tells us that He knows every intimate detail about us and He still loves us more than any of His creatures. We are of value to Him. He spends every minute of every day with us. He knows us and He loves us and this friendship with Him should be worth more than anything we possess. Walk with Him.

"Everyone who acknowledges me before others I will acknowledge before my heavenly Father."

MATTHEW 10:32

When I gather with groups I'm unfamiliar with, I become quiet in my Christianity. As I gathered with a small group of women one night following an awesome women's conference with wonderful speakers, I was asked what the "thing" I attended was all about. I only knew two of the women, so I casually blew off the day as simply a day to sell books that one of the speakers authored. Open door. Slam shut opportunity. The very next morning at Sunday Mass, the small voice whispered, "When the cock crows, denial." I immediately responded that I never denied Him. The small voice whispered, "If you acknowledge me, I will acknowledge you to my Father." And the small voice was completely on track.

Today and every day Jesus calls us to acknowledge Him. Simply acknowledge His existence, His work, His birth, His death, and His love. Not too much to ask. He knows and we know that many will roll their eyes and think, "Give me a break," but think of the deal He offers. For a simple acknowledgement He'll mention us to the Father. Our names will be spoken in the Heavens. On this day, speak His Name. The benefits are out of this world. Acknowledge Jesus.

May 7

"Whoever loves father or mother more than me is not worthy of me, and whoever loves son or daughter more than me is not worthy of me; and whoever does not take up his cross and follow after me is not worthy of me."

MATTHEW 10:37, 38

At the end of a weekend retreat I listened to a man share that his wife would be making the same retreat in the next few weeks and he was excited because it would be easier for her to understand why she was no longer "first" in his life. We all laughed. I happened to attend the closing of the wife's retreat a few weeks later where she blurted out to her husband in the crowd, "And you're no longer my first priority either!" The entire room burst into laughter. Of course, we all knew the feeling of putting Jesus Christ first and loving Him foremost.

Jesus calls us to love Him above all else. He also knows how difficult His request is because He gave us our parents, our spouse, and our children for this journey. He gives us these close personal relationships and yet He reminds us, Jesus first. He reminds us that He wants our relationships with Him to be one so deep with love that we will take up our own crosses daily and follow Him. He tells us this because He knows that we can understand that a full life with Him means so much more. Complete following of Jesus

Christ makes the rest of our relationships work. Above all, love the Lord Jesus. Jesus first.

 *May 8*

"And whoever gives only a cup of cold water to one of these little ones to drink because he is a disciple — amen, I say to you, he will surely not lose his reward."

MATTHEW 10:42

Great, simple ideas come when we least expect them. I helped a customer out with her packages one afternoon and as she popped her trunk I wondered where we'd fit her new bags. Although very organized, her trunk was full. She explained that she kept a small space with "brown bags" for those whom she may come across who are needy. I thought "Lady you could just hang around our parking lot all day and empty that space quickly." She had water and snack crackers for those she may meet hungry and socks and other small items for those who may have other needs. She was a traveling work of mercy and yet I thought what a simple, easy idea.

Jesus speaks to us about doing simple tasks for one another. He does not ask us to serve a seven course meal to a starving child. We do often tend to go overboard when asked to serve. He would rather us do one small act of kindness with the right attitude. He reminds us today that one cup can make a huge difference. Serve simply.

May 9

"Wherever you enter a house, stay there until you leave from there. Whatever place does not welcome you or listen to you, leave there and shake the dust off your feet in testimony against them."

MARK 6:10, 11

Many of us can probably think of places we have been that we never want to return. A bad experience in a restaurant or a store, an unpleasant time at a friend's house or in a certain city can bring about memories. In Europe I had a Eurail pass that allowed me to get on and off any train, anytime, anywhere. If I landed in a city and there was bad weather, I just got right back on the train and headed for a different city. If I wandered around and just did not enjoy the places suggested in the travel book, I caught the next train to somewhere else. I did not have to shake any dust, but I did need to keep moving.

Jesus gives us two messages. One is that He would like us to get out there and spread His good news. There are people everywhere who need to know how great a life they can have with Him. Full households and cities need to be reminded of His love. Secondly, we are to keep moving. We are to open our eyes and our ears and take time with one another, but if we fail in any way, we are to pick ourselves up and move on. He knows there are unpleasant times and places. Shake it off. Do not take it personally. Keep moving.

May 10

"Take nothing for the journey, neither walking stick, nor sack, nor food, nor money, and let no one take a second tunic."

LUKE 9:3

The task to take nothing on a journey seems impossible. Let's be honest. We can't go without a bag of some sort; an extra set of clothes, maybe a brush. When my daughter was going to Washington to March for Life, she was asked to bring one bag for several days. She managed to follow the request, but when I went to drop her off to meet the bus, I noticed one girl with several bags loading on before us. The girls all laughed about how this girl needed so much including her own bag of food because she was such a picky eater.

Jesus gives us a very simple message. We are all called on a journey with Him; men, women, and children alike. We are called, and He asks that we not drag the things of the world that will weigh us down. We all have baggage in our lives. Most of our baggage we have piled up ourselves or just allowed to pile up around us. Jesus tells us to let go of all this worldly stuff and journey with Him. He will provide for us; He will care for us; He will feed us. What holds us down is of our own making. Empty it all out. Take the chance. Journey with Him.

"Come away by yourselves to a deserted place and rest a while."

MARK 6:31

*A*fter the death of John the Baptist, Jesus tells the apostles to take some time alone. My older brother died at the age of 33, leaving behind a wife and two small children. I longed to be by myself. People mean well after we lose someone to death, but they really do not know what to say. They cannot help our emotions or cure our deep sadness, and sometimes in their need to make others feel better, they say inappropriate things. I did not want to go back to work. I wanted no one to talk to me or try to make it all okay. I should have found these words of Jesus and followed them. I needed to be alone and rest.

Jesus tells us to take some time alone. Whether we are in the midst of loss or sadness, or if we've been caring for others as most of us are always doing, we need a break. We do not always have to be on 24/7. First and foremost, we cannot do our best work when we are physically and emotionally drained, and secondly, we deserve rest. Today take time for yourself. Come away. Rest.

"Give them some food yourselves."

LUKE 9:13

*C*ountless times I have asked one of my children to get a younger sibling a snack or a cup of milk, and countless times they have found an excuse not to help. My response seems to always be the same, "Fine, I'll do it myself just like I do everything else around here." It's quicker to stop what I'm doing than to explain how much easier it would be if we'd all just pitch in a little. I'd be less tired, which would give me energy to do the extras they are always pestering me to do; take them shopping, to the bookstore, to the gym, or for a walk. Well, sorry, I'm too tired because I constantly have to get up and do every little thing for everybody.

We get the feeling that Jesus wants us to step up and serve one another willingly. He's here for us in case we really just cannot accomplish the task, but He wants us to try first. We are called each day to feed the multitudes that we come in contact with, and He suggests we break it down into smaller groups so the task will be more reasonable. There is no time for excuses. Give others what they need. Give of yourself.

"Gather the fragments left over, so that nothing will be wasted."

JOHN 6:12

$\mathcal{L}$eftovers. No matter how hard I try to cook just the right amount of food, it seems we always have some left over. It is great when my eldest daughter is home because it always gets eaten the next day. She will either have leftovers for her lunch or a snack, or both. Regardless, no food is wasted. But since she left for college, I'm afraid we have not been as good. She suggests a leftover night, which I remember my mom having as our family moved on in life; six nights of cooking to one night of leftovers. That will help us not to waste.

Jesus reminds us not to be wasteful. He tells us to gather even the smallest fragments for later. Take nothing for granted. Our society wastes so much, especially when it comes to food, and yet thousands starve each day. We must find a way to gather the fragments and share them with the world; whether it is literally food or clothing or time or spiritual gifts. Even the smallest leftovers in our lives can make a big difference to someone who has nothing. Waste nothing.

"Follow me."

JOHN 1:43

$\mathcal{I}$ love vacations. For many of us it still means some work planning and tending to children. Several times I drove six young children by myself from Nashville, Tennessee, to Naples, Florida, passing out drinks and snacks for fourteen hours and changing the occasional Barbie dress while steering through interstate construction. I may have been tired upon arrival, but it was still a vacation. For most of us, it is just time to be more relaxed and less stressed. When we arrive, someone else can be in charge or no one can be in charge and all is well simply because it's a vacation. It is time set aside to "get away."

Jesus calls us to let it all go. All the "we can handle anything." He says just follow. He will lead us. He will care for us. He will be our strength. He knows we are tired. He knows we can, but He says we do not have to do it all. We can just follow. We understand that following Jesus does not mean that we will be led down the easiest paths. We know by reading the stories where others were led that the road will not be easy. But we see and we believe that the end is worth the journey. The reward is worth the struggles. And if we truly let go and follow, we are led to a life filled with joys this world could never offer. We are called to take a vacation with Jesus.

<hr>

May 15

"Do not work for food that perishes but for food that endures for eternal life, which the Son of Man will give for you. For on him the Father, God, has set his seal."

JOHN 6:27

Green seal. Heat seal. Tupperware. We'll try anything to keep our food fresh longer. We push plastic tops down in the middle and lift the sides for a quick burp and voila, freshness sealed in. But if we do not use it, it cannot stay fresh forever. We seal our driveways and eventually, over time, they crumble away. We seal a deal with a hand shake and unfortunately, these days, we still know it probably won't last long. We seal our lips and ask our neighbors not to tell. Seals get broken. Things spoil.

God has set His seal on His Son. He is always fresh. His words, His life will last forever and never spoil. He is the food that endures for eternal life. This is what we look for in a seal. This is the freshness we long for in our food. Day in and day out we can rely on His seal, we can trust in His promises, and we can endure with His gift. Jesus Christ is forever.

<hr>

May 16

"This is the work of God, that you believe in the one he sent."

JOHN 6:29

When my husband and I first started the parenting process and our children were of the age to ask "Santa" for presents we taught them that they may ask for one gift. Some years it would be a Barbie, some years it would be a bike, but only one. They believed they would get that one gift "they always wanted." And there was nothing more rewarding than to see their faces when they opened that one gift. Granted, oftentimes we had to work a little and steer their choices to be more reasonable, but we came through none-the-less.

Jesus tells us that He is the one gift we are to believe. He is the one we've "always wanted." He is the one that when we understand His work and all He has done, and unwrap His gift to us, we believe without any doubt He is what we have always wanted and always needed. Truly joy can be found in one gift. All we have to do is believe. Want just one gift.

May 17

"Amen, amen, I say to you, it was not Moses who gave the bread from heaven; my Father gives you true bread from heaven. For the bread of God is that which comes down from heaven and gives life to the world."

JOHN 6:32, 33

I am always searching for the physical fix; the answer I can see and touch. My daughters and nieces went to the local Dominican convent to visit the sisters with my mother. On the "tour" of the new chapel as they approached the altar, the sister leading the tour proclaimed that Jesus was right there in the tabernacle. My niece logically asked the good sister how He had squeezed up small enough to get His whole body inside that little box.

Jesus point blank tells us that God has sent Him, and that He is the bread and He gives life to the world. No matter our mind's image of Jesus in the tabernacle, the truth we are asked to believe today is God sent Jesus. Within each Church, in every part of the world, Jesus is present, not because of the bread that man provides, but because of the Son that God gave. He comes and gives life. Squeeze some time for Him.

"I am the bread of life; whoever comes to me will never hunger, and whoever believes in me will never thirst. But I told you that although you have seen [me], you do not believe."

JOHN 6:35, 36

*R*epetition is a device used by public speakers to get their point across. Deacons and priests and ministers are often taught to say something and say it again and then repeat it for a third time. As I've read Jesus' words in the four Gospels over and over, I have come to realize the importance of this repetition. I have come to understand that it is not just fillers for an hour long talk or a ten minute homily. Repetition in the Gospels helps those who disbelieve that there could be a man who loves His neighbors, His friends, and His mother so much that He would give up His whole life for the sake of others.

Jesus repeats again that He is our Savior. He repeats the lesson that with true faith in Him we will never hunger and we will never thirst. How many times does He have to send His mother down? How many times does He have to gather saints in our midst? What more does He have to do for us to believe? And yet, He repeats Himself everyday in the Consecration. Partake. Believe again and again.

"And this is the will of the one who sent me, that I should not lose anything of what he gave me, but that I should raise it [on] the last day."

JOHN 6:39

I do not like to lose. I am extremely competitive, and most of the people who have ever played with me or against me in any sport know that basic fact. I know that fundamentals and practice are important to winning, and I work until each skill becomes a part of me or of whom I'm working. Fundamentals and practice are important in the fight to win in the spiritual life as well. Play to win.

Jesus tells us that it is His Father's will that we not lose. He knows we fear the loss of those we love and even the loss of ourselves to this world. He tells us this day that He will win over sin and death and we will not lose anything. It is the will of the Father that we all be saved. Know the basic fundamentals. Practice faith. Jesus saves.

"For this is the will of my Father, that everyone who sees the Son and believes in him may have eternal life, and I shall raise him [on] the last day."
JOHN 6:40

Generally, we like to see people succeed. We will our children to do well. Heck, sometimes I would bribe a child to work hard so they can succeed later. Meaning, if they will try basketball camp, I will buy them new shoes. If they will go to the gym with me, we'll stop for an ice cream treat later. However, they still have to believe in their own ability to succeed. They still have to put forth the effort to actually get the job done. We listen to the hopes and dreams of our children, and no matter how much we will them to accomplish their dreams, we can be forced to watch them fade because of lack of motivation.

Jesus speaks clearly of His Father's will for us to succeed. All we have to do is believe in His Son and we win. We need to motivate our children, our neighbors, and our friends, all whom we want raised on the last day, to simply believe. There's no room for lack of motivation here. The Father wills it. Believe and be saved.

"Stop murmuring among yourselves. No one can come to me unless the Father who sent me draw him, and I will raise him on the last day."
JOHN 6:43, 44

When I get angry I find myself murmuring about all sorts of things. In particular, I murmur when I think others should be helping out and they don't seem inclined. I murmur when someone hurts me unnecessarily and when life doesn't quite go the way I think it should. I murmur when I am asked to do something I really do not want to do. I murmur when I do not necessarily want others to hear what I'm saying. No one wants to be around me when I'm murmuring, and that's understandable to me.

Jesus tells us to speak up and to stop worrying about who is more important. His Father will draw us all to Him if we would just stop all the murmuring and get a grip. Jesus wants us to do His work, to get along with others, to let go of jealousy and anything else that keeps us from Him. If it's not worth saying out loud, it's probably not worth saying. Speak out.

<hr />

May 22

"Amen, amen, I say to you, unless you eat the flesh of the Son of Man and drink his blood, you do not have life with you."

JOHN 6:53

My mom, my two oldest daughters, and I rode with Adam, our driver, to a tiny little town in Portugal called Santarem. There we drove in circles and asked many locals where to find the church with the Eucharistic Miracle. Right smack in the middle of the town, down the tiniest roads I have ever ventured, was a dark little Church with only two people inside, but which held a mystery. Led behind the altar, we climbed one by one the steep narrow twelve steps to stand face to face with the flesh and the blood of Jesus. As in many places we visited in Portugal, Bl. Pope John Paul II had once stood in the same spot. We believe when we receive the Body and Blood because of our faith, but when we see the truth so close He can be kissed, our belief turns to indescribable.

Jesus reminds us that every day in Churches all over the world we are given the opportunity to eat and to drink. He comes to us in the form of bread and of wine, and He gives us life. Unless we go to Him and receive, we remain waiting. Say to Him, amen. Drive the narrow road. Find the Church. Make each day indescribable.

<hr />

May 23

"This is the bread that came down from heaven. Unlike your ancestors who ate and still died, whoever eats this bread will live forever."

JOHN 6:58

Forever I've heard myself say many times that I wish something could stay a certain way forever. I wish my children could stay young forever until they get older and do something more exciting, then I wish that time could be forever. The last day I walked down the center aisle of the Church I grew up in, tears rolled down my face wishing the structure would remain forever. I continued to look around and tried to paint an image in my mind so I would never forget. I thought I wanted that Church to remain that way forever, until we built the beautiful, large new Church where everyone can have a seat and all can feel welcome.

Jesus knows how hard it will be to let go of the physical world, so He offers us something everlasting. If we eat, if we partake, if we take into us the living, saving Bread from Heaven, which is Jesus, we will be with Him forever. For Him, it will not be until the next best thing or person comes along. He is ageless. He is timeless. He is forever.

May 24

"Do you also want to leave?"

JOHN 6:67

I well remember having slumber parties as a child. Oftentimes they weren't even planned, but it seemed that loads of girls just ended up at our house after a sporting event or a dance. Without fail, as one would leave, they would leave all. Without fail, the house would be empty in less than an hour, and I was left to realize that the fun was not about being with me but about being with the whole group. I agreed in my mind, because as the crowd dwindled to one or two, sometimes the talk became awkward.

Jesus asks us today if we will leave Him as others leave or if we will remain with Him regardless of how awkward it may feel. He knows we do better with others around. He knows being on His side can be a challenge, but He still beckons us to be with Him. No matter how many friends stop going to Mass or how many adults think they don't have time or how small the group is that we are left with, Jesus wants us to stay with Him. One on one. Just us. Stay.

May 25

"Hear and understand. It is not what enters one's mouth that defiles that person; but what comes out of the mouth is what defiles one."

MATTHEW 15:10, 11

$\mathcal{I}$t is odd that I often have to hop around on one foot because that other is so firmly planted in my mouth. "I didn't mean it that way." "That didn't come out right." "I wish I could take that back." We've all had the occasional slip. Words we speak and later regret. Once my older daughter let fly a curse word and my eight-year-old said, "Young lady, you know we did not raise you that way."

Jesus wants us to understand clearly that our mouths are what can get us in trouble. How we speak to one another and what we say about one another can make or break us. It is not about what goes in but what comes out. Use words wisely.

May 26

"O woman, great is your faith! Let it be done for you as you wish."

MATTHEW 15:28

$\mathcal{W}$ishes can come true if we just believe. "Star light, star bright, first star I see tonight. I wish I may, I wish I might, have the wish I wish tonight." How many times I've looked up into that sky filled with stars and made a wish! Even as an adult, just in case, I have closed my eyes and wished upon a star. We believe, especially as children, that those wishes really can come true.

Jesus says specifically to you and to me, let it be done as we wish. And of course, He wants us to believe. He wants us to have faith in Him. Not just lip service, but great faith. He speaks directly to us and tells us not to lift a finger; simply pray, have faith, and all will be well. As we wish.

May 27

"Let the children be fed first."

MARK 7:27

$\mathcal{E}$very meal together with our family begins with a blessing then the feeding of the children. We always get the young children their plates first. One by one they go around the table with an adult or a teen and have first choice of each dish. They are normally seated around the kitchen table and beginning to eat as the adults fill their plates and proceed to gather in chairs and on couches balancing food and drink and occasionally jumping up to check on the children. We could say that they are picky about what they eat so they need first choice. We could say that we are just wonderful parents. But truth is when the children are taken care of, our adult world is all good.

Jesus confirms our natural basic instincts. Feed the children first. Nourish them both physically and spiritually so they will grow in love and strength to take care of the world. Our hope is in our children. Our future is in our children. Feed them with the Word.

May 28

"Ephphatha!" (... "be opened!")

MARK 7:34

When my children were young and in the midst of other parents and children, if I corrected them and they did not obey, I'd say they had an ear infection. Their ears were so full of fluid, they could not possibly hear what I was saying. As perfect children, they would never just ignore me because they wanted to continue playing. Not my children. Must be the ears.

Jesus tells us to be opened. Open ourselves, our eyes, our ears, our mouths, our hearts, our souls, to the living God who wants to fill us with every goodness. Be open to the needs of those around us. Be open to offer our time and our service. Be open to love and to be loved. No excuses.

May 29

"My heart is moved with pity for the crowd, because they have been with me now for three days and have nothing to eat."

MARK 8:2

When the children of Medjugorje in Yugoslavia began having apparitions of Mary, thousands of pilgrims went to see and to hear and to pray. The small, remote village opened every door they could to accommodate the travelers. As one of those pilgrims, I was amazed at the hospitality of those who opened their entire lives to strangers. We were not sent away hungry by any means. Entire families "doubled-up" so we could have a place to stay. Children served meals to strangers. We were nourished physically, spiritually, and socially and the great distance was well worth the tough journey.

Jesus speaks of the importance of hospitality. He is always available to nourish us so we can continue, but He asks today that we feed one another, that we nourish one another from our hearts. Have pity on those in the crowd, on the street, in our community. Sometimes we may have to deal with a little inconvenience to ourselves or our families, but we are called to give from our hearts. Give them something to eat. Nourish them.

May 30

"If I send them away hungry to their homes, they will collapse on the way, and some of them have come a great distance."

MARK 8:3

I feel really bad when a customer drives a long distance to our bookstore and we do not have what they need. I realize they could have called first, and I realize we cannot satisfy everyone or carry everything, but it does not make me feel any better. I turn into my "need to fix things" mode immediately. First we try to substitute. Surely we have something on these four floors that can do or say the same thing as the product they need. If it is really specific, we offer to special order and to mail the item or call first, in case they are going to be near the store again soon. They have come a long way, and I work hard not to send them away empty.

Jesus tells us today to feed those who come to us. We encounter people for a reason. If we treated every encounter as if there was a purpose, we would work hard to satisfy. Many people go out of their way to come to us, to be around us, to visit. We are called to listen and to take care and to feed them, whether spiritually, physically, or mentally. Satisfy others.

May 31

"You of little faith, why do you conclude among yourselves that it is because you have no bread?"

MATTHEW 16:8

*T*here was a time at our store when our employees had little faith in the way my mom displayed. In particular, she would

98

make sure that the crucifix wall was organized in such a way that no small crucifix hung too closely under the cross bar of the extra large centered, focal point crucifix. About once a week, after she would leave for the day, the girls would go to the stockroom and gather a number of small crucifixes and hang them in the empty spots, concluding amongst themselves that this would bring about more opportunity to sell more merchandise. The cluttered choices never worked.

Jesus says that we prove to have little faith when we conclude things only amongst ourselves. He is the expert in our lives, and He knows what it takes to provide for us. We often gather together and make conclusions about all sorts of life situations. We know what's best especially as a group. Jesus says today to conclude only to have great faith. Decide.

June 1

"But who do you say that I am?"

MARK 8:29

When I first started working at St. Mary's Bookstore, I was in college. After college, I continued with the store, but as my peers asked me what I was doing with my life, I would always respond that working with my mom in the religious business was temporary. I wanted to open my own stationary or gift store once I learned the ropes. I did not want any of my peers to think that I was going to be hanging out in this Catholic bookstore for the rest of my life. I could not admit to others that I enjoyed who I was and the reason for my job.

Jesus questions our commitment to Him. He wants to know who we admit to. We have been saying in our prayers and in our hearts that we want to spend time with Him, that we need Him, and now He is calling us out. Who do we tell people we hang out with and enjoy spending time with? Do we admit that spending time with Him is awesome? Do we tell others that working for Him makes our day? Do we call Him friend, coworker, Father? Today, this first day of a new month, He calls for commitment to His work and to His name. Who do we say He is? Are we committed to Him?

"For the Son of Man will come with his angels in his Father's glory, and then he will repay everyone according to his conduct."

MATTHEW 16:27

Conduct! It seemed to always be my lowest grade. I know my conduct is ridiculous at times. Huffing and puffing and stomping around because I feel like I have to pull other people's weight. Often, it is not the situation that needs to be judged, but rather my reaction to the situation. You know, the typical how I handled my daughter forgetting her lunch, an employee having to leave early, or a neighbor clogging up my side of the creek with sticks and debris from his yard. The more I list, the more I realize that my conduct has not improved since grade school.

Jesus reminds us that there is definitely more and He is coming back for us. He wants us to know that we will be repaid for all the work we have done fixing lunches and working for others and showing compassion and ignoring the trivial. However, He will also repay us according to our attitude and our reactions in the midst of all our actions. How will our conduct affect our overall grade? Today we're reminded that it's not all about what we've done, but also how we've done it. What's our grade today?

"What profit is there for one to gain the whole world and forfeit his life? What could one give in exchange for his life?

MARK 8:36, 37

We make business decisions in our Christian store every day that help us work towards a profit to stay in business. If we gain, we generally reinvest back into the business to make it stronger and more stable for the months when there is no profit. In the long run, what profit is there if we have no business in which to act as prophet, as in to testify to the things of eternal life? A great exchange would be if we all used our profits to strengthen ourselves as prophets.

Jesus tells us that the world we put our energy into every day is worth nothing to us in the long run. We work hard to have and to give others, especially our children, the things of this world. Jesus wants us to work hard at the other word for profit. We can give our children and our coworkers and our community all this "stuff," but if we don't teach them what it takes to gain eternal life with Christ, we have given nothing. He wants us to reinvest in one another and make His world stronger. He will provide the profit. He wants us to provide the prophets. Make the exchange.

"O faithless generation, how long will I be with you? How long will I endure you? Bring him to me."

MARK 9:19

*H*appy medium. Oftentimes I feel like I baby my children. They bring home school projects, and I micro-manage every decision. They do quite a bit, but I give suggestions and trim edges and help to straighten pictures. I want them to learn to be responsible and to do their own work and I try to stand back, but ugh! — I just can't help myself. I know they need to develop their talents and the only way they will learn is if they practice. I know that I should have more faith in their abilities. I also know that I will not always be here for them and they need to learn to do things on their own. Children need to take time and to be allowed to be children, and they need to learn responsibility, and I need to learn to have faith in their abilities. There must be a perfect recipe some-where. I am continually praying to find just the right mix.

Jesus wants us to have faith in our abilities and the abilities of those we work with during our day. Those who we help will never learn if we manage every decision. We are not immortal. We must have faith in the next generation. Jesus tells us to learn from His example and be an example to others and continue the journey. We must believe in ourselves. We must believe in our children. We must use our talents to help others develop theirs so that we can persevere. Have faith.

"'If you can!' Everything is possible to one who has faith."

MARK 9:23

*I*f I worked harder I could attend a good college. If the coach had mailed those papers, my child could have gotten a scholar-ship. If I had been more enthusiastic, I could have a job I enjoy. If, if, if…. The slightest bit of doubt about ourselves or our abilities or the capabilities of others can alter our entire journey. Doubt holds us back and allows fear to creep in. My mother says "those who hesitate are lost" as she forges ahead in her positive manner. There is no room for doubt.

Jesus says, "if" nothing, "faith" everything. He calls us to believe. He calls us to have faith; in ourselves, in our coworkers, in our children, in our teachers and coaches, and in Him. Not just anything, but "everything" is possible. All our hopes, all our wishes, our entire journey hinges on faith. Grasp it. Cling to it. Keep it. And know that "everything" is possible. No doubt.

June 6

"If anyone wishes to be first, he shall be the last of all and the servant of all."
MARK 9:35

No longer first! It was difficult to swallow, but when I started having children I learned to give up all the firsts except the first to get up in the morning. First one fed, first to buy clothes or other needs, first to get a hug from Daddy, first to go to bed, and first to get attention from my own mom and dad. As grandmothers, as aunts, as teachers, as moms, as nurses, and as anyone else in service-oriented work, we all realize when we make the commitment that we are no longer first. Most every vocation we choose in life requires us at some time or another to put ourselves and our lives on the back burner.

Jesus tells us to accept our call because it will be rewarded. Every tired, aching moment of our service in this world will not go unnoticed. God first, others second, me last. We are called to be examples of true selflessness. No longer first with others now may seem difficult, but it's a small price to pay for eternity with Him. Be a servant.

June 7

"Whoever receives one child such as this in my name, receives me; and whoever receives me, receives not me but the One who sent me."
MARK 9:37

Many days I find it difficult for parents to shop in our store with their children. We have four floors so strollers are impossible for the most part. We have balconies over the front showroom that children love to run out on and wave to the customers down below. It makes the parents nervous, and yet for me and some of the other workers, it is a time to take care of the children while their parents shop. There is so much more in a child's life that they have to be careful about and that will seem fragile. When they are well received, talked to, listened to, read to, they tend to act fine.

Jesus tells us to welcome children. We actually have a natural tendency toward this and yet we often avoid the opportunities. We are busy. They are time consuming. And yet, Jesus says receive. We are all children of God so think like this. Every time we welcome one another, we welcome Jesus Christ. Live today with arms wide open. Welcome God's children.

June 8

"There is no one who performs a mighty deed in my name who can at the same time speak ill of me."

MARK 9:39

I am a Eucharistic Minister on Sundays and am occasionally asked to take the Eucharist to someone homebound or in the hospital. I know I am not worthy. There is no doubt that plenty of others in this world, in my community, are much more suited for the job. These words to John help me to get past myself. All I do is in the name of Jesus in the Eucharist and physically passing Him on to others is mighty indeed, but only because of Him, not me.

Jesus tells John to get over the fact that someone else doing good works in His name is not part of his group. Jesus is not concerned about who does the work, but that the work is done. He calls us today, and the sooner we get on board, the lighter the load will be for those out there working. He wants us to sign up. He asks us to do something in the name of Jesus and make this world a better place to prepare for the next. Do God's work.

June 9

"Do not prevent him, for whoever is not against you is for you."

LUKE 9:50

*F*ortunately, I have been to many sites where the Blessed Mother has appeared on earth, and I have given short talks about my

103

journey. Invariably after most talks someone asks, "What do you think about the sites that are not yet approved by the Church?" My answer is always the same. There are and always will be people in this world who just want to call attention to themselves. But there are apparition stories and sites that move thousands of people to conversion, to prayer, and to reconciliation, and who am I to worry about them or judge them? I picture our Mother storming Heaven and earth to save as many souls as possible, and if the belief in messages or visions turn people's lives around in these magnitudes, they must be good.

Jesus tells us that just because someone is not in our group does not mean they cannot bring others close to Him. He needs all the help on earth that He can possibly find. We know we have to be careful of false prophets, but at the same time Jesus says there will be others who know the truth. He asks us to work for Him and to not prevent others from doing the same in their own way. Bring others to Jesus.

June 10

"Salt is good, but if salt becomes insipid, with what will you restore its flavor? Keep salt in yourselves and you will have peace with one another."

MARK 9:50

I have noticed through the years of driving children to either participate in or watch various sporting events that the really good players we observe are those who play all year round. There are those natural athletes in the world who can join in a game at any time and play well, but the truly amazing players are those who are seasoned. Just as in learning a foreign language or a new computer program or whatever, if one does not continue to use and practice skills, he could possibly lose much of what they have.

Jesus tells us to continually keep salt within ourselves. We must be seasoned daily and rich in flavor, because if we lose what we have, it would take a lot to be fully restored. If we practice our faith and our love continually, then we will have peace. And, we could all use a daily dose of peace. Promote peace. Be salt.

"In just the same way, it is not the will of your heavenly Father that one of these little ones be lost."

MATTHEW 18:14

L ost. When I get lost, I tend to drive around until I luck into my destination. Makes my husband crazy. He wants me to stop and get directions, or even better, he would like me to get directions before I leave the house. I have actually gotten better with the use of the computer, but he still reminds me to stop and ask so I do not waste time driving and worrying about missing the event I should be attending.

Jesus tells us that it is His Father's will that each of us reach our destination. It is His will that no one is lost along the way. He wants us to get directions, to stay focused, and to follow Him on the journey so we do not waste time. The way will be much easier and we will not have to worry about missing anything if we understand the directions on the front end and follow them to their depths. Don't get lost.

"Again, [amen,] I say to you, if two of you agree on earth about anything for which they are to pray, it shall be granted to them by my heavenly Father. For where two or three are gathered together in my name, there am I in the midst of them."

MATTHEW 18:19, 20

A s my mother begins our morning in prayer at our store, she often says, "Lord, you say 'when two or three are gathered in your name,' and here we are. We ask You to be in our midst." This is why a four story Catholic bookstore has managed to flourish within the Bible belt. People frequently ask what a store like ours is doing in Nashville, Tennessee. We hope we are bringing others to Christ. My mother and others have prayed together and it has been granted by the Father. He is in our midst.

Jesus tells us that it is good to gather in group prayer. For us, it could be husband and wife, friends, family, Church, or work. It doesn't matter who; it matters that we are together and He is in our midst. Two or three in prayer. It shall be granted.

June 13

"I say to you, not seven times but seventy-seven times."

MATTHEW 18:22

True, complete forgiveness is not easy. Many times I think I've let go of a grievance or a grudge and it manages to pop up and cause a twitch months after the incident. I had a customer who bought several music CDs and wanted to return them a couple of days later after they had been opened. I was not happy with the exchange. He made a huge deal, gave the CDs to the other employees and proceeded to give each of them a little gift to prove what a great guy he was and how I mistreated him. I know. I know. Now, when he comes in, I just leave the area. He's probably long past the incident, but I cannot get over the way he makes me feel. An instant twitch.

Jesus understands that forgiveness is not easy. Of course, He never said that anything about this life is going to be easy. But He still has us go through it all. All the people who cause twitches, all the incidents, all the grievances are put in our paths to make us better. Forgive. Eleven times a day. Seven days a week. Let it all go.

June 14

"My time is not yet here, but the time is always right for you. The world cannot hate you, but it hates me, because I testify to it that its works are evil."

JOHN 7:6, 7

Good timing. When I backpacked through Europe many years ago, a priest in Germany encouraged my friend and I to go to Oberammergau to see the Passion Play. Performed every ten years, the chance for any tickets to be available was slim. But we journeyed. We had no place to stay, but asked a travel agent for suggestions. The man smiled and said that every place in town had been booked a year in advance. We explained that Fr. Thoni had sent us to this incredible place in these hills for an experience we may never get another chance to have. The man suggested we stay at his house. He could only offer a couple of pillows and blankets because he had no extra beds, but we were welcome. The next morning we walked up and down the long line of people, waiting at the closed ticket window, trying to find out if they were in line for the play. No one could answer our questions so when the ticket window opened, we walked to the front, stuck our heads in the window, and asked if we were in the right place. The man handed us two tickets and asked for money. The line gave a slight argument. We paid, we thanked, and we enjoyed the most amazing play we would ever see. The right place at the right time.

Jesus says that the time is right for us. We are not here to judge or to condemn, so we can take the burden off ourselves. We are here to watch and to listen. We are to simply journey and pray that our timing is right, and, when it is, to be thankful. Be there. Let Jesus handle the rest.

June 15

"Foxes have dens and birds of the sky have nests, but the Son of Man has nowhere to rest his head."

MATTHEW 8:20

I am lucky to have parents who have worked all their lives, nonstop, to provide for our family. They never expected anything to be handed them. They know that our time here is not about being at rest but about doing His work. Just when I thought they'd relax in their 70s, I find them in the chapel before the sun has risen, praying Rosaries, still going into their places of business and caring for children, grandchildren, employees, and customers.

Jesus tells us that work with Him is nonstop. He doesn't mean that we have to constantly worry about those in our lives. He'll take care of them. But He does ask that we be examples of His love and His trust and His life. We cannot slack off. The world is filled with temptation that tells us not to worry about time spent in prayer, at Mass, and following the rules. If we let down our guard, we might as well be like the animals who do not know better. Work for Him. Work with Him. Heaven will be our place of rest. Eternal rest.

"No one who sets a hand to the plow and looks to what was left behind is fit for the kingdom of God."

LUKE 9:62

The day after my mom bought our bookstore from the Diocese she began to move forward. She had the back wall cut in half to open the offices to the selling floor, which made the store feel larger. She bought new merchandise and began to plan for expanding. Two years later we moved into a four-story building a block from the Cathedral. After joining several organizations that supported our business, we were mailing catalogs to three states and she again planned for expanding. Today, we send catalogs to nine states, have five full-time employees and ten part-time employees. When I walk through that back door and she is there to greet me, I wonder where we're headed next. She has never looked back.

Jesus tells us that He wants our eyes forward, always looking ahead. As we work toward our goals, we need not worry about the past. We need to press on in a positive direction, always building, never tearing down. The past is gone and the future is bright. Our goal toward the Kingdom cannot be reached by wondering what we've missed. It can be achieved by working hard and moving forward. Plan to expand His work.

"Whoever speaks on his own seeks his own glory, but whoever seeks the glory of the one who sent him is truthful, and there is no wrong in him."

JOHN 7:18

I stood at the High School graduation of over a thousand students, and before the valedictorian spoke about his four years, he said, "First and foremost, I'd like to thank Jesus Christ. It is because of Him that I stand here today. Give the glory and the honor to Him." A roar went up in the crowd like I've never heard before in a large public setting.

Jesus warns us not to seek our own glory. All that we accomplish, all that we believe, all that we are is because of our God. Give Him alone the glory and in turn He will reward us. Think before we speak. Pray, so that what comes from our mouths is truth. Seek always God's glory.

"I performed one work and all of you are amazed because of it."

JOHN 7:21

We all have read different stories about saints and other holy people who have done one outstanding, amazing work and have changed something about the world around them. St. Maria Goretti's pardoning of the boy who killed her because she would not give in to his advances. St. Gianna Beretta Molla's sacrificing of her own life for the life of her unborn baby. St. Martin of Tours giving his cloak to the beggar. Bl. Pope John Paul II's forgiveness of the man who shot him. St. Maximilian Kolbe's volunteering to die in exchange for a stranger in the Nazi concentration camp. The man from our area arranging a funeral for the street guy who was hit by a car and killed. The teacher raising hundreds of dollars for the young boy fighting cancer. And the list goes on and on. One story that is told over and over because it has made a difference, an impact on the people who have witnessed or who have merely been amazed.

Jesus tells us that one work, performed completely out of love, is worth more than any long list of tasks. If we were remembered for one thing that we did today, what would it be? What have we done or what can we do to make a difference, to impact a life? We may only have this one chance. Make this day amazing.

"You know me and also know where I am from. Yet I did not come on my own, but the one who sent me, whom you do not know, is true."

JOHN 7:28

Times have definitely changed in our community. I once knew or at least recognized everyone in our neighborhood and our church and even our grocery store. Now, I only know the "originals." They are more the grandparents than the young families who are constantly moving in and out. Long lines of families don't seem to stay together in one area anymore, or so it seems, and understandably so in these times. People have to move where they can find work. As my coworker would quote from her mother who once knew or was kin to half of Nashville, "They don't know ya." Times have changed.

Jesus tells us that it is not difficult to know Him. We have a book about His life. We can hear about Him every weekend at Church. He wants us to know that there is more. By His life and His death and His resurrection, He has opened an opportunity for us. He wants us to know His Father. He wants us to know more than the "originals." He wants us to extend ourselves to everyone so even though some come and some go, and some "don't know ya," we can all be one community in Him. Know Jesus.

June 20

"I will be with you only a little while longer, and then I will go to the one who sent me."

JOHN 7:33

Time we spend with one another at the moment seems to linger, but in the blink of an eye it is over. A longtime friend of my father-in-law had planned to meet with him for lunch, and it happened to snow that day. The friend related that the last time he canceled an appointment with someone, the person died so he was going to make the meeting one way or the other. The friend said he walked to my father-in-law's place, 25 minutes each way in the snow and cold (sounds like a scene from their childhood), to have lunch and to visit. They talked about how happy my father-in-law was in his new place and how proud he was of his apartment. They talked about how well he was doing and how incredible the lunch menu was in the cafeteria. They talked about life. My father-in-law died unexpectedly two weeks later.

Jesus tells us to take time with one another. Life is just a little while longer for each of us. We are called to make the most of the time we have, every minute of every hour of every day. We will all someday have to go to the One who sent us. Jesus wants us to cherish our time together because before we blink, our little while is gone. Spend time together.

June 21

"Let anyone who thirsts come to me and drink. Whoever believes in me, as scripture says: / 'Rivers of living water will flow from within him.'"

JOHN 7:37, 38

$\mathcal{M}$anaging a Christian bookstore allows me to see customers every day who literally soak up any kind of spiritual writings they can get their hands on. We recognize them as genuinely happy. They are filled with a natural joy regardless of any hardships or tragedies they have endured. They find satisfaction in learning more from those who have gone before us or whose lives have experience. They constantly touch my life.

Jesus calls us each day to drink in the springs of life. Take a look and be open to the possibilities that well up around us. And in turn, we will have living water that flows and wells up in others. Drink it all in.

June 22

"Let the one among you who is without sin be the first to throw a stone at her."

JOHN 8:7

$\mathcal{O}$ur priest began his homily one Sunday following this passage with, "Then a stone came from the back of the crowd and popped the woman on the head. Jesus said, 'Come on mom! I'm trying to make a point here.'" His joke brought laughter, but also a reminder of Jesus' Mother's purity and sinlessness.

Jesus reminds us that we are called to help and not to judge. We are called to emulate His Mother in her purity and to work against sin. She is our model. Jesus knows we sin. He knows we are not perfect like His Mother. He forgives us and asks us not to sin any more. By His unconditional love, He makes His point. He doesn't have to pop us on the head although sometimes we could probably use the reminder. We are to judge only ourselves and ask for forgiveness. Strive not to sin.

June 23

"Woman, where are they? Has no one condemned you?"

JOHN 8:10

$\mathcal{I}$ sat in our Church one early evening with a crowd of others waiting for our deacon to review our tasks as Eucharistic ministers. After a brief prayer and overview, someone raised their hand and asked, "If we know a person is remarried outside the Church or only attends Mass on Easter and Christmas, do we refuse them Communion?" I think the deacon was as surprised as I was about the question, but simply answered, "We never judge or condemn." Then he went on to explain that our job is to feed those who come to the table and the state in which people receive is between them and God.

Jesus makes a strong point against peers condemning one another. His message, His food, His forgiveness, His love is for all. He came to save sinners, and when He asked today, "Woman, where are they?" that "they" is all of us. There is no one in our midst without sin. We are in the very popular majority where everyone is included and no one person is better than any other. And even He does not condemn, but forgives. Receive and be forgiven.

June 24

"I am the light of the world. Whoever follows me will not walk in darkness, but will have the light of life."

JOHN 8:12

*J*once made a retreat where a few leaders of the retreat asked a group of us to follow them. "Hold hands with one another and close your eyes." As we walked in darkness, we were told to duck and to stoop and to step over, and we listened and obeyed. After about 15 minutes and what seemed a lot of walking, we were instructed to kneel and to open our eyes. Before us was the tabernacle with one lit candle. In the darkness we were led to the light of life.

Jesus tells us that we must lead others on the journey to Jesus Christ. We are asked daily to help those He puts in our lives to duck and step over the debris of the world. We are called to teach trust and to lead through the darkness. We are challenged to bring others safely to the light of life. Take a hand. Lead another.

June 25

"You know neither me nor my Father. If you knew me, you would know my Father also."

JOHN 8:19

*M*y son and my husband could be twins if they were just born on the same day. We all know fathers and sons like these guys, who at some point look, sound, and act alike. It is uncanny, and yet I think it is interesting being around my husband in his childhood, so to speak. Oh sure, every now and then, he will say, "I don't understand. I never did that when I was his age." Well, no, but you aren't really the same people. God made each of them unique and yet knowing both somehow helps me to understand them both better.

Jesus says that if we knew Him, we would know His Father. They are one. Fathers can make a huge impression on their sons, oftentimes to the point that we see similarities in their voices and their actions. We are called to really know Our Father and to really know His Son so that we can better understand each one individually and as one. Know the Father and the Son.

June 26

"The one who sent me is with me. He has not left me alone, because I always do what is pleasing to him."

JOHN 8:29

Pleasing others. This is definitely important in our world of so many choices. I know in our retail store we find it necessary to be pleasing in our selection and our service more than ever before because of the convenience of the Internet. We keep customers strictly by pleasing them. I had a gentleman come in one day to buy a cross for his wife because he knew we would help him with his selection and then gift wrap it for her. We have several customers who call and place orders from out of town and then tell us about their families because we sincerely care. People want to be pleased. Like many other small family businesses, our store may someday be a lonely vacant lot if we don't take care of those who support us.

Jesus teaches us by example that we are rewarded for pleasing others. When we take care of the people He has placed in our lives, we please Him. When we take care of those who we meet by chance, we please Him. When we go out of our way to reach out to others, we please Him. And today, He tells us, we will not be left alone. He is with us always, right by our sides, because we are pleasing. His unfailing, unconditional love and constant companionship is our reward. Please Jesus.

"If you remain in my word, you will truly be my disciples, and you will know the truth, and the truth will set you free."

JOHN 8:31, 32

I have to say that sometimes in our lives it seems that a little lie would save us so much time and energy in explanations and arguments. Truth is it never works. Never. When I was in grade school, I told a group of friends that I disposed of a boy's ring to prove I didn't want to go steady with him. Truth is I accidently dropped the ring through a tiny hole where I could not get it back. I was embarrassed. I liked him and loved the idea of my first ring. The lie hurt the boy's feelings and ruined our friendship. One lie, no matter how tiny usually builds into something more before we can get it back and put it away. One lie leads to another. After a while, we need to ask ourselves, what is the truth?

Jesus tells us that He wants us to remain in His Word. He wants us to know Him. He is truth. He is life. He is the One who can set us free from all the ways of a world that's filled with pain and sorrow and confusion because of lies. Just as lies build into something more, so does truth. After a while, we need to know, He is truth. He will set us free.

"But you are trying to kill me, because my word has no room among you. I tell you what I have seen in the Father's presence; then do what you have heard from the Father."

JOHN 8:37, 38

*N*o room for words. I listened as a young mother told me of the diagnosis of her daughter's cancer. She explained the extreme procedures her daughter would have to undergo and the slight chance she had for a cure. I listened to the fear in her voice and the strength in her heart. I have learned never to interrupt an aching heart or a hungry soul. I listened even though I wanted to speak about hope and prayer because as we go through this life, we learn that in many situations, there is no room for words. After she finished, she said, "Will you keep her in your prayers?" "I will."

Jesus tells us there are certain times when words have no room in this world. The timing is just not right, and the word dies or falls on deaf ears. However, all that comes from the Father should be heard and put into action. The only way we will know what is right, is to listen. He knows we often hear the words while thinking of a response, but He wants us to listen and make room to hear His Father and follow His Word. Hear the Word. Make room.

"Why do you not understand what I am saying? Because you cannot bear to hear my word."

JOHN 8:43

We used to do this thing when we were young where every time someone would say something we did not want to hear we would plug our ears and repeat, "La, la, la, la, la...." The person trying to speak would do everything to get us to stop. They'd try to pull our fingers out of our ears, wave in front of our face, and finally just scream, "Please Stop!" Most of the time, the person with the message would give in and leave the room. How annoying! And yet, I still find myself plugging my ears when I cannot bear to hear what someone has to say.

Jesus tells us we need to listen to His Word. His Father did not go to all the trouble to send Him down here for us to ignore His teachings. Nothing He has to say is difficult to understand, but if we choose to plug our ears and let the noise of the world block His voice, then yes, we will miss the message and the life promised by the Messenger. We must pull our fingers from our ears, look at His face, and stop. Hear His Word.

"I do not seek my own glory; there is one who seeks it and he is the one who judges. Amen, amen, I say to you, whoever keeps my word will never see death."

JOHN 8:50, 51

I have a difficult time remembering that my life is just not about me. I love attention. Always have. And when I see an opportunity to jump in the limelight, I leap. Truth is it is never that good when I get there. For instance, the words I've been given in my writing. When I write what I think, the words are useless, bland, lacking. But when I pray about my writing, asking the Holy Spirit to guide my hand, I get feedback that truly speaks about the goodness of God. Every now and again, I will read something I have written and have to stop and think whether the words are mine or not. Guess they really are not mine. Truthfully, the only writing I have ever had rejected was all about me.

Jesus calls us to be like Him. He gives us an example to follow. He tells us not to seek self glory. This life is not about us, but rather about imitating the One who can save us from death. Jesus gives His all, and He wants us to do the same so that we will have eternal life. God our Father seeks us. He calls us to humble ourselves. He asks us to let go of all that is about us and turn it into all that is about Him. Give the Glory and the Honor to our God. Be humble.

July 1

"Neither he nor his parents sinned; it is so that the works of God might be made visible through him."

JOHN 9:3

One of my best friends died suddenly of a brain aneurism when she was only 33 years old. The young priest who celebrated her funeral explained her death in the most positive way possible. Jennifer did not die as a punishment to her or her parents, but rather because she was prepared. She had just bought a new condominium, and her old place was completely packed and ready for the movers. She had started going back to Church and was getting her spiritual life in order. She was made producer of a local news channel and played a pretty mean game of golf. We were not ready to let her go, but God was ready for her and His good works in her life were made visible.

Jesus assures us that bad things do not happen to us because we are bad. This is the way of the world. How we handle problems, challenges, and tragedies is what moves us and others closer to Heaven. We need to be prepared at all times to make the works of God visible. He is in control, and in His love and His mercy He will take care of us. It is up to us to keep our lives in order. Be prepared.

"Do you believe in the Son of Man?"

JOHN 9:35

Qs we grow in this world, we are often asked about our beliefs. Do we believe in magic? Do we believe there is a Santa Claus? Do we believe in ourselves? Do we believe in miracles? Many times we want to see to believe. We want to see the rabbit pulled from the hat. We want to sit on Santa's lap and receive the gifts we ask for. We want to accomplish something great. We want to witness a healing.

Jesus asks us a straightforward question. Do we believe in the Son of Man? We cannot touch Him although through prayer we can feel His presence. We cannot hear His voice although I believe many holy men and women have heard Him speak to them. We cannot see Him although we know His mighty works. Do we have the faith in our simple lives, sitting on our couches, preparing for our day; do we have the faith to truly believe in the Son of Man? We are challenged to take hold of that faith because that may well be all we need to make a difference. We are called to believe.

"I came into this world for judgment, so that those who do not see might see, and those who do see might become blind."

JOHN 9:39

J have gone to several mini retreats to try to get some extra hints or maybe easier ways toward salvation. Many times, as others have talked and asked questions, I have sat and thought, "I already know that. This may be a good refresher, but I didn't need to take the time, the night, the week." Well guess what? It was not organized just for me. And, news flash, maybe if I wasn't so sure that I knew it all already, I would get something totally different than I expected.

Jesus explains that He does not just come for those who already have it all, or so they think. He comes to those of us each day that need to be saved by Him. He is here for those of us who realize that we need Him and those who do not realize the need. He wants us to wake up and not be so sure or too self-assured. He wants us to humble ourselves, and as we do we will probably get something totally different than we expected. Be open. See.

"When he has driven out all his own, he walks ahead of them, and the sheep follow him, because they recognize his voice."

JOHN 10:4

I attended a college retreat because I was asked to support the speaker by supplying books that she wanted to suggest for the attendees. I have to say it was four incredible nights of learning. The speaker's intent was obviously to build leaders. There was not one person in charge that I did not recognize as a Christ-bearer. These kids follow Christ, and in turn we recognize Him in them and we want to follow Christ too. Attendance was high because there was an attraction. Their happiness, their sincerity, their Christianity was contagious.

On this day of our celebration of Independence, let us recognize the need for good Christian leadership. We know that those who "walk ahead" are only as good as who they follow. If we see Christ in them, then we can see their goodness and strength and sincerity. Jesus says to follow and to recognize His voice so that we can recognize the truth in others. Recognize Him. God Bless America.

"A hired man, who is not a shepherd and whose sheep are not his own, sees a wolf coming and leaves the sheep and runs away, and the wolf catches and scatters them. This is because he works for pay and has no concern for the sheep."

JOHN 10:12, 13

*T*he occasional difficult customer can make our employees in our bookstore call for help and then scatter upon our arrival faster than fire. We have had our share of those who yell about a price or a product or an inadvertent comment from an employee. There is just something about an angry Christian that intimidates. But for those of us who are in it for the long haul and want to keep every customer, with the belief that something we serve them will turn them around, we view difficult customers as potentials. This is our livelihood. They are a part of our life. We are interested in them all.

Jesus tells us that we are His whole life, and He wants to be ours. He has a vested interest. Nothing in this world is bad enough to separate Him from us. He sees our potential, and what He has to serve will keep us together. He is truly concerned. He wants us all. We are called to be concerned in return. We are called to gather.

July 6

"I have other sheep that do not belong to this fold. These also I must lead, and they will hear my voice, and there will be one flock, one shepherd."

JOHN 10:16

*I*n the neighborhood where we grew up, with the exception of a few yards and a few houses, there were no fences and families rarely locked their doors. The place was open to all, and all were welcome, especially, in our house. With eight kids already, what were a few more? Our house was appealing to the other kids. The havoc, the hecticness, the rules, the Christianity of our parents, the blatant love of all — it did not matter if one didn't actually belong, we were all one and all were welcome.

Jesus calls us to ecumenism. We are called to open ourselves to others and let them see what life is like with Jesus as Our Father so they too will come to the fold. This should be our daily prayer. No fences. Open doors. One fold. One shepherd. All are welcome. Yes, there are rules and the occasional chaos, but the love received is worth all the work. The life given and shared is appealing to all. We must remain open.

July 7

"Go on your way; behold I am sending you like lambs among wolves."

LUKE 10:3

I have a tiny little mother, and for some reason, the largest, boldest, meanest street people lower their voices around her. The toughest men I know speak softly in her presence. I feel like the world would eat her alive, and yet she wanders through not just fine, but on top of things. She is a lamb among wolves, but the Holy

Spirit is so obvious in her that the wolves dare not trod. Her love for others is sincere and God help anyone who offends or hurts the ones whom she loves.

Jesus says that He knows we are often thought of as meek. He knows we are often timid. He knows we are the underdog. But He also knows we are just what this dog eat dog world needs. He made us this way because the world needs kindness and tenderness and love. We are called to go on our way, the Jesus way, "like lambs among the wolves." Be the lamb.

July 8

"Whoever listens to you listens to me. Whoever rejects you rejects me. And whoever rejects me rejects the one who sent me."

LUKE 10:16

When my husband and I first began raising our children, we corrected them with the idea in mind that they needed to do the right things so that our lives would be easier. As time passed, we realized the mistake in our approach. We have been around enough young people to understand that we need to teach all children to listen and to obey because it is God's law and it will in the long run make their lives better. It's really not about us at all.

Jesus tells us that the messages sent from Him are to be passed on and accepted, not to make the messenger's life easier and better, but because it is right for God. It's not our message, our success, or our rejection. It is so that we can pass on and accept the saving power of God. If we listen and get it, we can pass it on. If we reject the message, we reject the messenger. Then what? We'll be trapped in a world all alone with others around us stuck in rejection and failure too. Listen. In the long run, our lives will be better. Accept the message.

July 9

"Nevertheless, do not rejoice because the spirits are subject to you, but rejoice because your names are written in heaven."

LUKE 10:20

I have a tendency to get pretty pumped up after a talk or a workshop where I have given any kind of insight or helped in any way to provide what others have come seeking. I stand next to Jesus and say, "Hey, this is cool." When I pray for the Holy Spirit to guide my words and my actions, others not only listen, but they share and agree. I see nodding heads and smiling faces. I can easily get wrapped up in the moment.

Jesus tells us just because we've come to know Him and our life is good on earth and we make people happy, we still need to concentrate on the work that wins us Heaven. Feeling good about our work is one thing, but having our names noted in Heaven is another. We must do His work to win in Heaven, not just on earth. Rejoice. We are called to let go of instant gratification. Strive for the Heavenly reward.

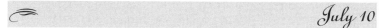

July 10

"I give you praise, Father, Lord of heaven and earth, for although you have hidden these things from the wise and the learned you have revealed them to the childlike."

LUKE 10:21

*W*hen I was a child, I loved when the Sears catalog arrived. A plethora of toys and clothes were revealed that I never would have known existed. Those who had most everything didn't need to see the "wish book," but I scoured over the massive volume for weeks. I would fold down the edges of certain pages I wanted to go back to and cringe when other family members wanted a turn to "shop." Regardless of how often I went through that book, each time I reopened it, I found something new that I thought I could not possibly live without. Of course, it held "more for your life."

Jesus tells us that we need to be open at all times to learn something new. After all, we are His children, and He has much to reveal to us if we are willing to listen and learn. As our lives change week after week, we should start each day ready for something new. We should walk with our eyes and ears and hearts wide open. There is so much more. We are called today to continually reopen ourselves to the One we cannot possibly live without. Listen and learn.

"Blessed are the eyes that see what you see."

LUKE 10:23

I am one fortunate child of God. He has blessed me with many opportunities and has given me the means and the ability to take those set out in front of me, for the most part. I have witnessed young and old share moments of faith. I have seen believers crawl upstairs and around the sites of the apparitions of Mary on their knees praying the Rosary. I have seen the eyes of the sick cured and the work of those who serve change the lives of those they encounter. I have been shown, I have been touched, I have been strengthened, and I have been moved. I have seen the work of God in children, in teens, in adults, and in almost every religious denomination I can name. I can truly say that my eyes have been blessed.

Jesus tells us to open our eyes to one another and see what He sees. Only through this encounter will we have the opportunity to feel the power of Jesus through one another. The eyes speak. They tell our story. He wants us to treat others as if they are the only ones in our life at this time. He wants us to witness what is happening and strengthen one another with our faith. He wants us to be open to see and to take the opportunities set before us. We are challenged to really see. Be blessed.

"Which of these three, in your opinion, was neighbor to the robbers' victim?"

LUKE 10:36

*E*yes wide open. That's the way we must walk through this busy life as to not miss any opportunities. When our store was located in downtown Nashville, every day to and from work I would pass by homeless, hurting men and women who sometimes I would hand the change from my pocket and sometimes I would pass hardly noticing their needs. As I drove home one day, stopped at a traffic light, I looked to the corner on my right and saw a man, waiting to cross, whose face was covered with blood. I mean covered. My heart screamed at me to roll down my window and hand that man the towel on the seat next to me. On the seat next to me!

Just roll down the window. And yet in my fear, as the light changed, I drove past him. For weeks, I could see the man's face, and not in a haunting way, but in a way that reminded me over and over of Veronica wiping the face of Jesus. It reminded me of an opportunity for yet another person in a chance meeting, awarded a sign, to show compassion. Would the towel next to me have the imprint of a face that could be my ticket to heaven for simply showing compassion? I think not. But a missed opportunity? Absolutely.

Jesus asks us if we will be the one who does the right thing. Will we stop and take care of the victim? Will we be a true neighbor? Throughout the busy day, we may just need to stop long enough to look someone else in the eyes as they speak and offer them hope. One moment. One hour. One day. Who will we be?

"Martha, Martha, you are anxious and worried about many things. There is need of only one thing. Mary has chosen the better part and it will not be taken from her."

LUKE 10:41, 42

J tend to make myself keep busy around tough encounters. My husband, Allen, and I have a good friend who developed a life-threatening illness. Allen had gone by the friend's house at the request of his son, and by early morning he was following an ambulance to the hospital. Suddenly, this man was not expected to live. I called a friend and we went and cleaned his apartment. Through many surgeries, through coming in and out of consciousness, through hearing awful prognoses, my husband sat by his side, even when his friend did not know he was there. I went back and cleaned out the refrigerator. The minute we heard about the miracle of his recovery, Allen continued to be around him, and I went for one last cleaning. Allen chose the better part.

Jesus calls us to sit with Him and to listen and to spend time. We often keep our lives so busy that we forget how to just be. Jesus wants us to stop being anxious and worried. He wants us to know that He is the One thing we are in need of, and we must choose Him. He is here, and He will not be taken from us. Spend this time with Him.

"Father, hallowed be your name, / your kingdom come. / Give us each day our daily bread / and forgive us our sins ..."

LUKE 11:2–4

When I entered first grade, I had a rough start. We began our day by praying the Our Father, and I cried and cried completely out of control. So much so, that my sister had to be retrieved from her class to calm me down. The prayer overwhelmingly reminded me of home. It reminded me of my father.

Jesus teaches us today to pray, and not just any prayer, but the prayer that helps us connect to the Father. He wants us to ask daily to be fed, to be forgiven, and to win salvation. And in return, all He asks of us is to forgive everyone in debt to us. He tells us in His words today that if we simply forgive all others what they owe us, we will not be subject to the "final test." The gift is before us. Let us pray.

"I tell you, if he does not get up to give him the loaves because of their friendship, he will get up to give him whatever he needs because of his persistence."

LUKE 11:8

We believe that Our Blessed Mother, Mary, appeared to a simple peasant, Juan Diego, in Mexico City, Mexico, in 1531. My favorite lesson on persistence comes from St. Juan Diego. During those appearances, after he tries to dodge another encounter with Mary, needing to get help for his sick uncle, he stops and he listens and he goes once again to deliver Mary's message. He continually and persistently delivers her message until he finally convinces the local bishop and the world that Mary has appeared to him.

Jesus speaks to us of the importance of persistence. Persistence in our homes, persistence with our children, persistence at work, and persistence in prayer will make a difference. Continually asking. Continually thanking. Continually seeking. Jesus is persistently pursuing us. He will give us whatever we need because of our persistence. We are called to continue His work. Be persistent.

"If you then, who are wicked, know how to give good gifts to your children, how much more will the Father in heaven give the holy Spirit to those who ask him?"

LUKE 11:13

*E*ach Christmas our family puts our names in a bowl, and each person picks one to buy a gift to exchange on Christmas Day. The whole point is to strive to know the person a little better by talking to a spouse or a child about what the person has been up to or in to for the year. The idea is to keep us connected. We joke about putting names back of those most difficult to buy for and hoping that certain ones choose your name who have bought great gifts in the past. On Christmas Day, there's nothing better than opening one well thought out good gift. One good gift is truly what is used, what is appreciated, what is cherished, and all that is needed.

Jesus tells us that those who ask, will receive the Gift of the Spirit. The Gift will be more than any of the greatest gifts we have received. The Gift will keep us connected to the Father. If we ask, we will receive all we need to make it in this world . One great gift, the Gift of the Spirit, is all we need. Receive God's gift.

"Whoever is not with me is against me, and whoever does not gather with me scatters."

LUKE 11:23

*A*s often as possible, and for every reason she could think, of my mother gathered our family together. On Sunday, we went to Mass as a family of ten. For dinner, we gathered at the table all together. When we went on vacations, they were family vacations. She wanted each and every one of her family members on the same page. She wanted us listening to the same words, eating the same food, nourishing ourselves with the same Bread, and enjoying one another. Before we were too old, all going our separate ways, scattered all over, my mom wanted to give us each the same foundations. She knew we would be a stronger force in this crazy world if we were all for one another.

Jesus tells us today that it is vitally important for us to gather. In our homes, in our churches, in our prayer groups, and in our communities, we build strength in numbers to keep us together against evil. We must gather with Jesus. We must join with Him in all facets of our lives, and we must stay together. We are called to begin in our own families and reach out to others. We must gather.

July 18

"Rather, blessed are those who hear the word of God and observe it."
LUKE 11:28

When I looked up the word blessed in the dictionary, the definition included "favored." We have always joked around about one or another of our siblings being my mom's favorite child. Well it was probably the one at the time who would listen to her and obey her requests. When I started having children of my own, I found myself favoring the ones who did what I asked them to do simply because it made my life run smoother. Truthfully, they are all my favorites, but there is just something about everyone doing what needs done that keeps down the yelling and the arguing and the wear and tear on the parents. And it's the simple things like taking up their laundry and putting their dishes in the dishwasher and cleaning their rooms. It is all the things that if they do not do them, I have to do them. Yes, I am blessed to have each one, and I know it, but I could swing toward favoring the ones who listen and do what's asked.

Jesus tells us that we all can be blessed. Merely follow two requests. Hear the Word of God and observe. I know deep in my heart that He "favors" every one of us, but in my mind, I would like to be the favorite child. Who wouldn't? We are called today to be blessed, to be favored, to hear, and to observe. Be God's favorite.

July 19

"This generation is an evil generation; it seeks a sign, but no sign will be given it, except the sign of Jonah."
LUKE 11:29

I love it when I feel I have been given a sign from above, a confirmation to go ahead with or to halt what I'm doing. My arms fill with goose bumps. Plus, it makes me feel right about the final decision. After my father-in-law died, his children arranged a memorial at the funeral home, and my husband was asked to get someone to say a few words. Upon leaving the family meeting, the funeral director told him that the deacon from our church was asking about him. We looked at one another and said, "There's a possibility." Not being able to get him on the phone, I was about to suggest another speaker. Suddenly, in walked our deacon to our bookstore to drop off a project for me. I couldn't miss the sign.

Jesus stands in our midst a might bit perturbed that we continue to ignore all the signs. Jonah was three days in the whale, and Jesus was three days in the tomb and the shroud was left as proof. So the sign that He died and He rose and He dwells among us is the flashing light. It should cause the goose bumps. Jesus is real. His message is for today. We are given the word to follow. Be aware.

July 20

"The lamp of the body is your eye. When your eye is sound, then your whole body is filled with light, but when it is bad, then your body is in darkness."

LUKE 11:34

My mother has to have a prism in her glasses to correct her vision. One summer, my two older girls and I traveled to Spain with my mother without those glasses. Jesus' words were confirmed day after day. "The lamp of the body is the eye." My poor mom was miserable having to cover one eye to see anything. She became physically sick and had to actually stay in the hotel some days. Thank goodness she had brought her portable paints so she could capture some of the beauty of the cities on canvas off her balcony. She made the most of the sight she had, but her body was definitely "in darkness."

Jesus warns us to take care of what our eyes see because they control what our body does. The evil in this world can physically bring us down. He wants us to make the proper choices and keep our vision clear and see the beauty of His creation. A body in darkness is miserable. Cast off darkness.

"Although you cleanse the outside of the cup and the dish, inside you are filled with plunder and evil."

LUKE 11:39

y husband and I used to joke around and tell our kids that we didn't care how they acted inside our house, but once they set foot out in public they had better act right. In the car, when riding to certain events, we would usually give everyone a little speech about proper behavior. And we would have to remind the younger ones not to mention that they had been given a speech. Of course we truly want them to love one another and act right inside and out, but if we have to choose....

Jesus calls us out. He sees right through us. He tells us point blank that He doesn't want us to just look like we're holy; he wants us to be holy. Inside and out. He wants us to do the right things. Live a good life. Confess what's in our hearts and be cleansed. Jesus calls us to be holy. Reject evil.

"Woe to you! You love the seat of honor in synagogues and greetings in marketplaces."

LUKE 11:43

uilty as charged. My intentions are not always in the right place. I love it when I know everyone in the room. I love it when all eyes are on me. Not too long after I graduated from college, I was asked by organizers at my high school to come one night and help call donors for the annual alumnae giving. Ugh! Calling people and asking for money! But it was for my alma mater so I agreed. I couldn't just show up and do the job — I dressed up in my old high school uniform, sodality pin attached to bolero and all, and got quite the laughs for a night that I thought would be grueling. We told old stories and new stories, and every once in a while someone would come around the corner to my desk to show a newcomer what I was wearing. It was a fun night.

Jesus says woe to me! Needing the spotlight and all the attention is not what we need. The focus, the spotlight should always go directly back to Him. If we truly live the Christian life, we would reflect Jesus. He would get the honor and the credit. We would shrink so that He could be seen. Today and every day, may all we do honor Him. Let others see Jesus.

"You have taken away the key of knowledge. You yourselves did not enter and you stopped those trying to enter."

LUKE 11:52

*C*ollege dorm rooms and apartments are not the greatest places to get school work done especially when we have to study for tests or write papers. Someone in the group always seems to have nothing to do but have friends over or play loud music or want to talk. I spent many nights sitting outside in the hallway studying while my roommate needed to sleep "with no lights on please." Occasionally now I get calls from my children complaining that they have to "live in the library" to get anything done. Ahh, those were the days with their love, hate relationships and the complete, utter selfish behavior of groups of peers. Those were the days of searching for just the right roommates only to find that no one was really on the same page. At some point, most everyone is guilty of keeping others from learning.

Jesus says that we can not only keep ourselves from learning, but can prevent others from trying to learn. We do not know everything. We don't have it all. There is so much more, and we need to be open not just for ourselves, but also for others. He wants us to stop being self-centered. He calls us to think about others and the impact our lives have on their lives. Be open to learn.

"There is nothing concealed that will not be revealed, nor secret that will not be known."

LUKE 12:2

I often wonder if my husband would marry me all over again knowing what he knows now. When we dated, I wore plenty of makeup, fixed my hair just right, wore different clothes, and held back many of my oddities. He didn't need to know everything right away. I thought I should grow on him first. Let him discover that I'm not great about putting away the laundry. I don't care about getting my oil changed the minute the sticker on my windshield says it's time. I like to drive around the parking lot and park close to the door I need to enter. I do not care for directions or instructions. I don't mind wandering through back roads and down highways until we find our destination. I don't care if plans change or we decide at the last minute to go somewhere because I love to be spontaneous. Seems once we married, the concealer started to wear off. Now twenty-seven years later, the secrets are all out and I have to wonder if he'd do it all again.

Jesus says we might as well lay it all out in the open on the front end. He knows our every move. He knows our heart, and it's best just to be honest. We can hide nothing from Him. He loves us and He forgives us and He will always take us back. Lay it out there. Regardless of the years, He loves us even knowing what He knows now. Be open.

July 25

"Take care to guard against all greed, for though one may be rich, one's life does not consist of possessions."

LUKE 12:15

I pay very close attention to children and teens. Their actions and their reactions often teach more than any classroom could ever hope. I see them absolutely have to have the latest craze just to move on to the next "thing" upon its possession. "Oh my gosh mom, we have got to get …" is a typical statement at our house. We have bought cell phones only to find out that the "must have" feature caused the most problems. We have bought cameras and Game Boys and iPods only to hear of an amazing upgrade on a newer model. We have bought jeans that have been worn twice. The truth is they don't really need "things." They really need love and attention.

Jesus says to us that our life is not made up of what we have. Who we are truly has nothing to do with what we own. We can have everything in the world, but if we do not love we are nothing. We are called to let go of the "things" so our arms are free to hold another. Jesus is our "must have." He is the best feature, fully loaded, always upgraded. Don't be greedy.

"You fool, this night your life will be demanded of you; and the things you have prepared, to whom will they belong? This will it be for the one who stores up treasures for himself but is not rich in what matters to God."

LUKE 12:20, 21

*B*efore I backpacked through Europe, one of the Dominican sisters at my high school gave me the address and phone number of a priest living in Germany and told me that he would be glad to give me a place to stay if I made it there. Well, He did much more than just provide a place to stay. Fr. Thoni drove us down the autobahn, through the back streets of small towns to see a Maypole, and took us to meet a true shepherd. We visited an old walled city, and he treated us to the most wonderful German meals. His motto is that he can't take it with him so he might as well spend it on what he enjoys. I could not have been more grateful.

Jesus tells us that collecting wealth in this life is completely worthless. What matters to God is our love for one another. All else is temporary satisfaction and can be lost in an instant. More of us should live our days knowing that "We can't take it with us." We are called to prepare for what matters to God. Store up God's treasures.

"Therefore I tell you, do not worry about your life and what you will eat, or about your body and what you will wear. For life is more than food and the body more than clothing."

LUKE 12:22, 23

I wake up each morning and wonder about what I'm going to wear and what I'm going to have for dinner. Those are the two things I am constantly thinking about, food and clothing. Call it the way of the world, call it the way I was raised, call it what you want, but I cannot seem to shake the habit. My mother grew up in a house where three women stayed in the kitchen preparing meals from morning to night. If they weren't cooking, they were sewing, and they were thinking about cooking. She said when the first meal was finished and the kitchen cleaned, preparation for the next meal began. For these women, it was their way of life during times of struggle, but for me it's just my struggle.

Jesus reminds us that He will take care of our basic needs in life. If we follow His lead and do what is expected of us, of course, we should not worry. Now, just as the bird has to go and get the food that the earth supplies, we too have to make an effort, but it does not have to be a struggle. It is all here for us. We are called to have faith in the One who truly provides. No worries.

July 28

"Instead, seek his kingdom, and these other things will be given you besides."
LUKE 12:31

Each month at our bookstore we write a financial goal for sales on the calendar. We strive for an amount that will help us not only stay in business, but thrive, so that we can meet the needs of our customers and serve them well. The goal is not simply to survive, but to offer a store stocked well with the work that God wants us to pass on to others. We know it's easy for people to get on the Internet and buy what they want, but we hope those who come through the store are blessed with the goodness and the peacefulness they need. We hope they find what they came for and get a little extra for their efforts. When we focus on obtaining the goal, all His work seems to come together naturally.

Jesus is point blank. We must seek His kingdom. Our focus must be in getting the One thing that we are here to obtain. As we go through life, as we wander, as we search, He will provide us with the little extras along the way. We will be blessed. Today we are to focus on His kingdom and let everything else come together naturally. Accept the challenge. Receive the gifts.

July 29

"For where your treasure is, there also will your heart be."
LUKE 12:34

I know I have watched plenty of movies based around the main character spending his entire life in search of some rare treasure. The lost ark. The pot of gold. The buried treasure. The goblet, the stone, the jewel, the secret. Many of these stories end with the character finally getting the "treasure" only to find empty promises. They find that the true treasure has always been right inside them. The answer was there all along, in their hearts.

Jesus says today that what we treasure, what we value the most, will be what we do or strive for or love with all our heart. If the things of this earth are what we treasure, then here is where all our effort will be rewarded. But if our real treasure, that rare jewel buried deep in the heart of all we do, is Jesus, then all our effort will be rewarded with Him. We are challenged to find the priceless gifts He has to offer. With all our heart.

July 30

"Be sure of this; if the master of the house had known the hour when the thief was coming, he would not have let this house be broken into."

*I*f I only knew then what I know now." We'd all love to have a little hindsight to save us from regrets we've had to face in our lives. I wish I had tried a little harder in high school and thought more about what I wanted to do with my life. I wasted a lot of time settling into my vocations. I wish I had known to spend less time thinking about life as a chore and more time enjoying every task set in front of me. I wasted a lot of time learning it's not all about me. I wish I had spent more time with certain people. But we must learn to let go of the "what ifs" and the "wish I hads," because at some point we realize that this is all just a part of living. The sooner we let go of our uncertainties and our regrets, the sooner we can get on with the best part of life. I think we know what we need to know, but we may just need to let go and let God take the lead. He knows.

Jesus says to be prepared for what lies ahead because this life is uncertain. He does not want us to live in regrets. He does not want us to come to the end of our lives worrying about all the unknowns from the past. He wants us to prepare every day for our eternal life. We do not know when the end will come, and today we are asked to live each day to the fullest. Jesus does know and He challenges us to let go and to follow Him. No regrets.

"Blessed is that servant whom his master on arrival finds doing so."
LUKE 12:43

At work, we don't play boss and employee, or master and servant. I know the boss and I know the master. I try to stress working as coworkers. But it never fails that anytime I walk down the stairs or around the corner, my younger workers scurry to get busy doing something as if I am going to get angry about them goofing off. I'd just love the time to come when we all just did our work because we get paid to do our work and because we enjoy serving others. What a truly blessed atmosphere our places of work would be if everyone just did the right thing. We would be able to spend a lot less time monitoring and a lot more time working to make this world a better place.

Jesus calls us to be blessed. He wants us all just to follow the Gospel message, do what we are asked, love one another, and be blessed. He doesn't want us just to do the right thing when He's watching or when others are checking in on us. He wants to find us faithful and prudent. Then, He will give us more responsibility. Then, we will be blessed.

"I have come to set the earth on fire, and how I wish it were already blazing!"
LUKE 12:49

I enjoy a nice fire in the fireplace or outside in the fire pit on a cool night, but I'm not the best at building a good blaze. I try sticking rolled up newspaper under the logs and adding plenty of kindling, but the flames always seem to smolder. One night as I was shoving in kindling like crazy, some sparks popped out onto the carpet and before I could stop it, made a large black mark in the lovely green shag. I have learned to use starter logs, which help the wood to ignite and burn better than anything else I've found.

Jesus reveals His desire that this earth be on fire with His Spirit. He came to ignite us, and He wishes for us to not just keep the flame alive but to make it blaze. Roll the newspaper, add the kindling, or break down and buy the starter logs if we have to, but set this earth ablaze with His Spirit. Set the earth on fire.

August 2

"You know how to interpret the appearance of the earth and the sky; why do you not know how to interpret the present time?"

LUKE 12:56

*I*n these times of advanced technology, meteorologists can practically predict any type of weather. Now, granted, Mother Nature still has the handle on the severity of the weather, but we can see a lot of what's coming our way. The appearance of the sky can make all of us take notice. Dark clouds, high winds, and torrential rains make us seek safe places. I never mean to scare my children, but after seeing what damage bad weather can cause, I have had them move to the lower most interior rooms of our house more than once.

Jesus questions our interpretation of the world around us. He knows we can read the signs because we do so with the weather. He wants us to look around. He wants us to see the levels of poverty, the abuse, the war, the evil, and He wants us to interpret what it means to close our eyes to it all. We are called to go to the lowest most inside places. Seek safe places so that as we do for others, it will be done for us. Read the present time.

August 3

"Why do you not judge for yourselves what is right? If you are to go with your opponent before a magistrate, make an effort to settle the matter on the way; otherwise your opponent will turn you over to the judge, and the judge hand you over to the constable, and the constable throw you into prison. I say to you, you will not be released until you have paid the last penny."

LUKE 12:57–59

*W*hen we first opened our bookstore, an elderly lady fell on our steps and broke her wrist. My mother took her to the doctor, and we drove the woman's car home. She had no one to take care of her. My mom checked on her several times and took her to her appointments until she was well enough to take care of herself. She probably could have made a big issue over her troubles, but there was no need because my mother did what was right. The lady did what was right. Accidents happen, but people still need to take care of one another.

Jesus tells us to settle matters before they get out of hand and people get angry. We wouldn't spend billions of dollars a year in court fees and lawyer fees if people simply treated one another with kindness and respect the way they themselves wish to be treated. Spite and hatred ruin lives. Do what is right. Take care of one another.

August 4

"Or those eighteen people who were killed when the tower at Siloam fell on them — do you think they were more guilty than everyone else who lived in Jerusalem? By no means! But I tell you, if you do not repent, you will all perish as they did!"

LUKE 13:4, 5

$\mathcal{A}$ woman who once worked with us at St. Mary's Bookstore surprised me one day by expressing her fear of flying. She is petrified to fly. She has a wonderful spiritual life. She prays and she attends Mass regularly. She has a great devotion to our Blessed Mother. I could not fathom her fear, and so I asked her why in the world she did not trust that God would not take her unless it was her time. Her answer was quick and to the point, "Well, now, what if it's the pilot's time and I just happen to be on the plane?"

Jesus tells us to repent and to always be ready. We do not know the hour He will call us, and if we are not always prepared, we could perish with the rest of the group. When we are vigilant, ready, repentant, then even if we do go when we least expect it, we do not "perish" but rise to eternal life. Jesus calls us to continual repentance. Be ready.

August 5

"'Sir, leave it for this year also, and I shall cultivate the ground around it and fertilize it; it may bear fruit in the future. If not you can cut it down.'"

LUKE 13:8, 9

I am the mom of second chances. Call me crazy, but I believe that many times a simple lack of self-control, a slip up, a mistake in judgment, deserves another try. "Let me have one more try. Just one more try, and if I don't get it this time, you can take it away." I can hear the begging. Let me have my bike back just one more time. Let me drive your car one more time. Let me go out with my friends. Let me get on the computer. Everyone wants another chance if they've messed up or been slack the first time around.

Jesus is giving us another chance at a deeper Christian life. He gives us another try at nourishing with His Word and at planting the seeds of His love so that our future, our children will continue to bear the fruit of His life. We must work to cultivate good. We must work to bear good fruit. Let us try this again. This year. This day.

August 6

"Hypocrites! Does not each one of you on the sabbath untie his ox or his ass from the manger and lead it out for watering?"

LUKE 13:15

A priest friend once explained to me that there are certain tasks that must be done on the Sabbath to prevent harm from or to help others. For example, he has to preach on that day and attend to certain needs in his parish. Unavoidable. So, he is careful to take other opportunities during the week for his day of rest. He keeps holy the Sabbath, but his seventh day, his day of rest actually falls on a different day. We wouldn't want to let the outside world get to us, but we can all think of people who need to attend to the cares of others on the Sabbath; doctors, nurses, firemen, ministers. But I have to say, wouldn't it be nice if restaurants and retail stores were closed so everyone just stayed home with family and friends?

Jesus tells us not to be too literal and yet not to let the ways of the world into our spiritual beliefs either. If someone needs ministered to or healed or fed or nurtured, of course we need to attend to them; even on the Sabbath. As long as we do not fall into the trap of trying to work all the time for the world and for ourselves instead of for our souls, we will not be called hypocrites. Contemplate your schedule. Plan according to your needs. To the needs of others. To His ministry.

"What is the kingdom of God like? To what can I compare it? It is like a mustard seed that a person took and planted in the garden. When it was fully grown, it became a large bush and 'the birds of the sky dwelt in its branches.'"

LUKE 13:18, 19

𝓝ot long ago I toured the house where we grew up. I went directly to the girls' bedroom where the closet was exactly as I remembered. I think the paper lining on the shelf was the same as when we lived there in the 1960s. The boys' bedroom was different because the zodiac on the ceiling had been covered over with white paint. I wondered as I passed from room to room how we all fit into that tiny space. Ten of us lived there, but most days there were many more. The neighbors tended to visit and to stay, whether just for coffee and talk at the kitchen table or to spend the night. To me, it never seemed crowded or too small, until this day of my return.

Jesus tells us that as we nourish one another, as we grow together, we become much like a seed that grows to be a large bush where all come to dwell. In our space, in the places of our hearts, all are welcome, and all who come tend to stay. As the kingdom of God is planted in the hearts of His people, those who come together tend to stay. All dwell together in the hugeness of His love. All are welcome.

"To what shall I compare the kingdom of God? It is like yeast that a woman took and mixed [in] with three measures of wheat flour until the whole batch of dough was leavened."

LUKE 13:20, 21

𝓜y sister's cinnamon bread is awesome. She swears it's an easy recipe, but the minute I saw the words dough, rise, and fold, I knew I'd leave the "easy" to her. Unfortunately, I do not have the patience my sister does to mix dough and wait for it to rise. These days I grab a tube out of the refrigerator, whack it on the side of the counter, lay dough on a cookie sheet, and bake. Guess I could even "fold" some cinnamon between the dough if I want to get fancy. I admit that I had to look up the meaning of leaven, which means to cause to rise, to permeate with an altering or transforming element.

Jesus compares the kingdom of God to the yeast that makes all the difference to the outcome of the whole batch of dough. It can rise and permeate and transform or it can be set aside and the whole batch can flop. We are called to incorporate all the ingredients. We are called to spread the kingdom, to rise to the occasion. To be transformed.

August 9

"If I do not perform my Father's works, do not believe me; but if I perform them, even if you do not believe me, believe the works, so that you may realize [and understand] that the Father is in me and I am in the Father."
JOHN 10:37, 38

No doubt, actions speak louder than words. I can preach to my children about the importance of a relationship with God, but more than that I need to show them the importance of that relationship. I can explain to my children about the importance of healthy eating and exercise, but unless I make the salad and take them to the gym with me, it means nothing. I need to exercise and eat right so I am believable. The same can be said for being an example of reading and going to Mass, being kind to others and doing service work, and joining prayer groups.

Jesus tells us today that even if we cannot see Him or hear Him or believe Him, we can still see the proof of His work. The results of His works are all around us. We are called to realize and to understand. His actions are loud and clear. Look around. Look closely.

August 10

"Strive to enter through the narrow gate, for many, I tell you, will attempt to enter but will not be strong enough."
LUKE 13:24

Small entrances are always intriguing. We visit my sister in Hapeville, Georgia, and love to eat at the original Chick-fil-A, known as the Dwarf House. When my children were young, they were fascinated with the tiny Dwarf door through which they could enter. Of course it was their size and a place where adults would not necessarily venture. When we visited Rock City, their favorite places on the trail were the needle's eye, fat man's squeeze, and the swing-a-long bridge. As you can imagine, those are all the narrowest paths where only one person can fit through at a time and some wondered if they could fit through at all. But we all wanted to see what was on the other side so we sucked it in and moved along the trail. The little children had no problem, but I had doubts for myself. Funny how those roads seem to narrow a little more as we age.

Jesus calls us to strive to come to Him despite the narrow entrance. He calls us to be strong in a world that is unforgiving. He calls us to walk a path that few can walk. He calls us to follow a way that others dare not go. The opening is narrow and all that is good lies just ahead. Each day, He calls us. Strive to enter.

August 11

"For behold, some are last who will be first, and some are first who will be last."

LUKE 13:30

I can picture my mother's face low into my face saying, "Honey, not everyone can be first. Someone has to be second and third and last." And I remember thinking, "But not me. I need to be first." I have always been competitive. It must have something to do with being number six of eight children. However, when I started having children, I understood my mother was right. Surprise. Surprise. Not everyone can be first and not everyone is last, and in the overall picture, where we are in the line right now will make no difference. Our place in this life will not matter in the next, but how we handle our place, our calling in this life, will matter.

Jesus speaks to us about the kingdom of Heaven. He tells us not to worry about our position in this life. What we should care about is how we treat those who are first and how we treat those who are second and third and last. What truly matters is how we handle ourselves and others. We are called to be at our best. In our own place.

"How many times I yearned to gather your children together as a hen gathers her brood under her wings, but you were unwilling!"

LUKE 13:34

There is absolutely nothing I like better than to have all my children home. I even prefer them all to be together in the same room. Or better, to all be crammed into my daughter's SUV. After the initial "You're touching me" or "Tell her to stop pushing on my seat" is over, we can enjoy just being together with all our similarities and all our differences. Everyone at some point says, I don't want to be together, but once we are, they love it.

Jesus tells us that He wants to keep us all together. We are the ones fighting with one another, unwilling to let go of our petty differences. He yearns for us to be with Him. In His arms is where He prefers us all to gather. He outstretched them on the cross to prove His love, and all we have to do is let go and fall into them. Keep together.

"Rather, when you are invited, go and take the lowest place so that when the host comes to you he may say, 'My friend, move up to a higher position.' Then you will enjoy the esteem of your companions at the table."

LUKE 14:10

We, as parents, grandparents, aunts, uncles, Christians in general, are used to this idea of taking the lowest place. We take the seat in the car that no one wants, the last place at the dinner table, the middle seat on the plane, the edge of the bleacher, the chair instead of the pew during the Christmas-Easter seasons or Chreaster, as a friend pointed out to me, and sometimes, with no place left at all, we stand. And here is our confirmation that having to take the least desired seat can oftentimes land us in the most desirable places.

Jesus confirms that it is much better to go ahead and take the place that no one else wants than to be embarrassed and asked to move or have someone make a scene. We all know what climbing over one another to get a seat looks and sounds like in a parking lot, in a sporting event, at a dinner, and especially in the Church pew.

Jesus tells us today to humble ourselves and trust that in the end we'll all get a better seat. Take the lowest place.

August 14

"Rather, when you hold a banquet, invite the poor, the crippled, the lame, the blind; blessed indeed will you be because of their inability to repay you. For you will be repaid at the resurrection of the righteous."

LUKE 14:13, 14

I had many girls in my grade school who always invited the entire class to their parties. They, or at least their parents, wanted no hurt feelings, no one left out. Whether or not these girls would ever be invited to the others' houses in return did not matter. They invited everyone anyway, and their parties seemed to be the most fun. They were truly kind. Many of us could never repay or reciprocate all the parties and dinners throughout our years together, but that is not why we were invited in the first place.

Jesus tells us to purposefully do for those who cannot repay. Those who do not have, those who cannot pay, the ones who cannot walk or talk or see clearly, and all who come in need are the ones for whom we need to work, to care for, and to love. The children, the homeless, and the aged need us to give without expectation. When all are satisfied, we will gain our reward. Welcome everyone. Be kind.

August 15

"A man gave a great dinner to which he invited many.... But one by one, they all began to excuse themselves.... Go out to the highways and hedgerows and make people come in that my home may be filled. For, I tell you, none of those men who were invited will taste my dinner."

LUKE 14:16, 18, 23, 24

*M*any of us have had employees or coworkers or children who seem to have an excuse for everything, even when it isn't necessary. I'm late because.... I took extra time because.... I need to leave early because.... I can't come to work because.... At times, we've all wanted to scream, "I do not want your excuses, I want you to do the right thing!" If they're late, make up for it and call. If they need more time, stay late or let someone know. If you need to leave early, then come early. If you can't work, get someone to take your place. But please, stop giving all these excuses!

Jesus tells us that when He sends us an invitation, as He does daily, He doesn't want our excuses. He wants us. He wants us to come to Him in the morning and be with Him in the day and stay with Him through the night. This is why many pray the divine office, one of the structured ways to answer God's continuous invitation. We are called to let go of all the excuses. Join Him.

August 16

"Which of you wishing to construct a tower does not first sit down and calculate the cost to see if there is enough for its completion?... In the same way, everyone of you who does not renounce his possessions cannot be my disciple."

LUKE 14:28, 33

Everything costs more than I expect. While having a '63 Ford Falcon restored, my husband and I had no idea what it would really cost to finish the project. Plus, we had no concept what it would be like to keep her in good shape year after year. More than we expected. Many of us start projects that tend to take more time than we expect. Even taking time to write a book of 365 meditations was a stretch for me. Do we plan to make it to the very end? Do we have enough? Enough time? Enough talent? Enough energy to actually finish?

Jesus tells us that He wants us to calculate what it costs to give up everything so that we can be with Him in the end. He doesn't want part of us now and nothing later. He wants us to complete the task, to finish the race, to be with Him at the end of this project. He wants all. Every day. Every month. Every year.

August 17

"I tell you, in just the same way there will be more joy in heaven over one sinner who repents than over ninety-nine righteous people who have no need of repentance."

LUKE 15:7

A priest friend once asked me, "Who am I that I do not need forgiven?" As I have aged I realize what joy repentance brings to my life. I have never really liked confession. I felt like I could walk in and say the same words each time. But true repentance, true confession, and the feeling of absolution bring me joy. My heart, my soul, my entire being feels free. Lighter. Half my life I have avoided the very thing that brings true peace. Now, as I leave to do my penance, I feel the smile shoot across my face and know that the same joy is being felt in heaven.

Jesus confirms the answer to what the priest asked me. No one is too good for repentance. We need to be forgiven. We need to confess to our wrongdoings, to our faults, to our imperfections. And in return we will know complete joy. We are called to repent. Called to be free.

August 18

"Or what woman having ten coins and losing one would not light a lamp and sweep the house, searching carefully until she finds it?"

LUKE 15:8

One morning our family realized that our dog was out of the fence. She was terrified of storms, and we guessed that in the middle of the night there must have been sounds that scared her enough to want to run. We called, we searched, and finally we received a call from miles away to say they had found our dog. There is no doubt we could have gotten another dog if Heather had never returned, but we wanted her. We wanted our lost dog.

Jesus teaches us the importance of bringing home the lost. Light the lamps, sweep the streets, carefully and meticulously search, because each one lost must be found. Each member, each child is important enough to drop all we're doing to bring back home. Jesus wants the one that is astray to come back home. He knows there are many others, and he loves them. But right now, He wants the lost. Focus on the lost.

August 19

"And when she does find it, she calls together her friends and neighbors and says to them, 'Rejoice with me because I have found the coin that I lost.' In the same way, I tell you, there will be rejoicing among the angels of God over one sinner who repents."

LUKE 15:9, 10

$\mathcal{F}$ound money. I have many times in my life reached into the pocket of a jacket, a coat, or a pair of pants that I have not worn in a months and found cash. Sometimes a little and sometimes a lot. I'm reluctant to let my children know this for fear they may start searching the pockets of the clothes in my closet! But I do not hesitate to gather them and take them for ice cream or some other treat in celebration. After all it was money I never counted on.

Jesus shares with us the same rejoicing over one sinner who repents. He knows what it means to find what has been lost, no matter how much or for how long. The point He wants us to focus on is complete celebration over even the least amount. He wants each and every last one of us to come back to Him. Rejoicing among the angels. Now that's a celebration.

August 20

"My son, you are here with me always; everything I have is yours. But now we must celebrate and rejoice, because your brother was dead and has come to life again; he was lost and has been found."

LUKE 15:31, 32

$\mathcal{M}$y younger children joke with me when the older two come home from college and I spend the first month of summer doing everything they want. I make what they want for dinner or go eat at restaurants they choose. I know that time with them is precious and short. Although they can come back and visit, it will not be the same. The spoiling is short-lived, but it does seem to happen.

Jesus tells us that if we have been with Him all along these trials of life, what He has is already waiting for us. But even if we have strayed, He wants us back, and when we arrive, there will be one huge celebration for all to attend. Rejoice and celebrate with Jesus because our time here is just a short visit. He is constantly calling us home. Time to celebrate.

August 21

"The person who is trustworthy in very small matters is also trustworthy in great ones; and the person who is dishonest in very small matters is also dishonest in great ones."

LUKE 16:10

When finding someone to watch over her children, my neighbor started by having my daughter watch her younger children while she completed chores around the house. Soon she found herself able to leave my daughter with the children while she went out and ran errands. That slowly moved from thirty minutes to hours at a time. Someday she'll be able to leave her children with my daughter if she needs to leave town as I have with my sitters in the past.

Jesus wants us to gain His trust. He wants us to take care of one another, one person at a time until we slowly build up His kingdom. He wants to trust us with small relationships that grow and with small tasks that mount. Jesus trusts us with His work, one person, one encounter at a time. We are challenged to be honest. Even in the smallest matters.

August 22

"No servant can serve two masters. He will either hate one and love the other, or be devoted to one and despise the other. You cannot serve God and mammon."

Luke 16:13

Our bookstore was started by the Diocese of Nashville in the 1940s to provide families with good reading material to aid their spiritual lives, rosaries for prayer, and crucifixes and statues and medals as reminders of Jesus, Mary, and the saints. Occasionally I get completely wrapped up in the world of the worldly. I get so involved in completing tasks that I forget to serve. There are plenty of gimmicks in the marketplace that I could buy to make money for our bookstore. And believe me, I know I need to stay in business, but whom do I really serve, the maker of the product or my Maker? Does the item turn people to Jesus? Not everything. No doubt. But we try to stay with items that bring others closer to Him.

Jesus is firm and precise. He gives no choices, and He never says some of us can handle two masters and some can't. He is definite. We are to serve God and God alone, and all else will be taken care of through that choice. We are asked to stay in line with what will keep us closer to Him. Today and every day, make choices that serve God alone. Choose God.

"You justify yourselves in the sight of others, but God knows your hearts; for what is of human esteem is an abomination in the sight of God."

LUKE **16**:15

I have a friend whose wife is not easy to get along with at times. I try to make it a point to say something nice about her in the midst of the struggles regardless of how I truly feel. But basically, she can enrage me. This is a huge failure for me. She is a child of God, and I should be able to let all else fall by the wayside, but it's just one of my failures. Whenever I say something to one of our mutual friends, she says, "It is okay to talk to me about her. You have to vent to someone." But actually, the whole situation makes me feel bad.

Jesus says He undoubtedly knows. I can justify the talk as a way to vent if it makes me feel better, but it still doesn't make it right. I don't need to vent. I am gossiping, and we're all just thinking of ways to make it okay. He knows my heart. And in these cases, He says it is an abomination in His sight. We are told today not to justify the ways of this world. God knows.

"It is easier for heaven and earth to pass away than for the smallest part of a letter of the law to become invalid."

LUKE **16**:17

I had to pick up speed coming down the hill to make it up the other side." The officer never missed a beat as he wrote out my speeding ticket. "Ma'am, the law's the law. If I let everyone with a great excuse go without a ticket, there might as well be no laws, and then there'd be tragedies and recklessness and havoc all over the place." "Yes sir, but...." "But nothing. Everyone is expected to obey the law."

Jesus tells us that every part of the law is to be obeyed. Even the smallest parts we may find easy to wiggle around and the parts that society suggests we overlook. We can easily see the tragedies and recklessness in our world today. This life is full of havoc. Jesus says obey the law. Even the smallest part. Excuses will not be accepted.

"'My child, remember that you received what was good during your lifetime while Lazarus likewise received what was bad, but now he is comforted here, whereas you are tormented.'"

Steve often sleeps under our back alcove at our business. He has a set of twins and a wife, but he can't seem to straighten his life up to care for them. He drinks entirely too much alcohol, and yet the help we offer is refused. But we still offer in hopes that one day he will accept. Maybe one day he will come from the depths of his torment and save himself.

Jesus warns us that all the riches of this world will pass away, and we will be judged by how we treat one another. A lifetime of happiness on this earth cannot compare with what He has in store for us in Heaven. Give to those in need. He wants us to prosper so that we can assist those who are less fortunate. Sometimes the very one we need to help is right at our feet. We are called to care for others so that our Heavenly Father can repay us in the kingdom. Comfort the tormented.

"Things that cause sin will inevitably occur, but woe to the person through whom they occur."

I was always considered a leader in school. Not so much because people looked to me for direction as much as I was loud and opinionated. Channeled correctly, I could be an asset, but the possibility that I may lead an entire class astray was of concern to many of my teachers. I once had my whole class convinced that turning on the air conditioner and opening all the windows in the dead of winter would make our English teacher crack up laughing and postpone half our class time. I was wrong, and the entire class suffered.

It is safe to say that Jesus wants us to avoid anyone who could lead us astray. He does not want us to sin, and He is specifically hard on those who drag others to sin. He knows how easy it is for us just to follow the crowd, especially one that seems loud and crazy, but He wants us to watch out for these people. They can bring us all down. Avoid sin and those who delight in sin. Lead not others astray.

August 27

"If you have faith the size of a mustard seed, you would say to [this] mulberry tree, 'Be uprooted and planted in the sea,' and it would obey you."
LUKE 17:6

Small people making big things happen. We oftentimes hear stories of the youngest or smallest member making the biggest impact in a family's walk of faith. A simple word can shake things up. A small request can make a large impact. A fight for life against all odds can change everything. Bl. Mother Teresa of Calcutta, a woman small in stature, made a huge impact. Lourdes, Fátima, Guadalupe — tiny, remote villages where we can find many deeply touched by the faith of the people who live there and those who come to visit.

Jesus tells us that if we have the smallest amount of faith, true faith, big things can happen. With God on our side, we can make a difference. If we want to be heard, if the message is worth repeating, if lives are to be changed, we must remain small so God can be seen. It is not about size. It is all about faith.

August 28

"When you have done all you have been commanded, say, 'We are unprofitable servants; we have done what we were obliged to do."
LUKE 17:10

I am a numbers person. I love to work with numbers at the bookstore and figure out if certain product is pulling its weight in comparison to the place it occupies. Knowing obviously helps us decide where to spend money. Truthfully, when it boils down to the bookstore, it's about service. That's our obligation: to serve our customers. Those who walk in are more important than the money they leave behind. Now, we know we have to run it like a business to stay in business, but we also know we are called to provide what will keep or turn others to faith, to serve our community, to reach out, to tithe, and to pass on the gifts we are given.

Jesus calls us to embrace our obligations. We know His commands. We don't have to have the best of everything, nor do we have to be poor, but we are to serve the rich and the poor. We are to love those who get on our last nerves and those who we do not yet know. We are to gather and to plant. We are to listen and to follow. At the end of each day, we are to sit back and say, "Hey, we have nothing to show for ourselves, but all You sent us are taken care of and we have fulfilled all the obligations You set before us." Follow His commands.

August 29

"I am the resurrection and the life; whoever believes in me, even if he dies, will live, and everyone who lives and believes in me will never die. Do you believe this?"

JOHN 11:25, 26

When I was about eight, my dad drove our family, including my grandmother, from Nashville to California to visit Disneyland. What a trip! Eleven people in a station wagon pulling a camper. Disneyland was amazing to me. I paired with my grandmother and discovered after many rides and much walking that she was lost. She had no idea where the rest of our family was or how to find them. She was worried most of the day while I had no idea. I believed in her, and I felt safe. I was having the time of my life.

Jesus calls us to believe and live. He has done the hard part. He has gone before us. He has made the path much easier to obtain a life that will never end. We are simply called to believe in Him and to follow. As we rise from sleep and begin our day, we are to have faith in the One who died and rose again to save us. We are called to believe.

August 30

"'Father, I thank you for hearing me. I know that you always hear me; but because of the crowd here I have said this, that they may believe that you sent me.'"

JOHN 11:41, 42

At the bookstore, it seems I have the same challenges over and over with the new employees. In the mornings, I oftentimes have a little meeting and tell everyone what I need a few to hear.

"Hey guys, let's remember to stop having conversation with one another while there are customers in the store. They will not interrupt you to ask for help." "Remember to check on customers after they have been here for a little while." "Do not talk about customers or anyone else, especially while others are in the store, joking around or not." Words said to everyone to benefit a few.

Jesus reminds us first of the importance of praying to our Father and that He will always hear our prayers. He also tells us, He has come to earth so that we may believe. He does everything for our benefit. His Father sent Him for us, and we are called to give thanks. His Word speaks to the crowd. For the benefit of all.

August 31

"Ten were cleansed, were they not? Where are the other nine? Has none but the foreigner returned to give thanks to God?"

*I*t never fails that when any of my children have friends over, their friends seem far more grateful for everything I do for them. I get thanked for food served and for rides given and for movies rented. I get thanked simply for allowing them to come to my house. I love having their friends come over because I am reminded that my small tasks are appreciated. I am sure my children are just as grateful to other parents when they stay with their friends.

Jesus tells us that oftentimes outsiders appreciate the gifts given in a community more than the locals who tend to take them for granted. He wants us to return to Him. He wants us to be grateful. He wants us to be cleansed. He asks us today to return and give thanks. Give thanks to God.

September 1

"The coming of the kingdom of God cannot be observed and no one will announce, 'Look, here it is,' or 'There it is.' For behold, the kingdom of God is among you."

LUKE 17:20, 21

*M*any times in my life I have wished I had known what was about to happen. I could have been prepared for the simple

151

pop quizzes and the unexpected deaths. But nothing brings this passage home like the flood of 2010 in Nashville. In an instant, businesses were destroyed, lives were lost, and families were left homeless. I watched as thousands rallied around complete strangers and removed debris, served food, clothed, listened, and prayed. We witnessed "the Kingdom of God" among us. Words could not explain what occurred in Nashville better than Jesus' words today.

Jesus tells us that the Kingdom of God is among us. It is not one "thing" to be pinpointed. The kingdom is in the lives we touch, in the way we work, in the people we meet, and in the world we care for. It is this and more. So the one we cut off in traffic or let in and the one who drives us crazy or keeps us on track and the one who ruins our day or whose day we ruin — all are a part of God's Kingdom among us. As we move through our day, may we all treat His Kingdom like a Kingdom. Serve one another.

September 2

"The days will come when you will long to see one of the days of the Son of Man, but you will not see it. There will be those who will say to you, 'Look, there he is!' (or) "Look, here he is.' Do not go off, do not run in pursuit."

LUKE 17:22, 23

In my younger days, I watched the TV show *Charlie's Angels*. Three young women were given instructions from "Charlie," a man they'd never seen, to catch "bad guys." At the end of each episode, the girls would arrive at a place where they had "just missed" seeing Charlie. Truth is, we all wanted to see him, but if we did, the show would be over, the mystery extinguished, the game won. As episodes continued, how the girls solved the crimes was exciting, but waiting to possibly "see Charlie" held me to the end of the show.

Jesus tells us to stop looking for someone or something in this life to save us. If we keep running after the "next best thing" of this world, we will waste our time and our energy. These heroes of today can make us feel good, but they cannot ultimately save us. We keep searching and seeking, always in pursuit of the next fix of happiness, and it can be exciting, but it certainly can't help us in the end. Jesus satisfies.

"On that day, a person who is on the housetop and whose belongings are in the house must not go down to get them, and likewise a person in the field must not return to what was left behind."

LUKE 17:31

I sat glued to the television as rescue workers repelled from helicopters and saved victims of Hurricane Katrina stranded on their rooftops. They waited knowing that when they returned, if they returned, they would have no possessions, but they would be saved. As we all know, many of them could not go back, and not everyone was fortunate enough to escape death.

Jesus tells us to leave our possessions behind and move forward to the One who will save us. We are not to think about what we have worked for on this earth because that is the baggage that will eventually bring us down. Let it all go and move on. He is the hand that rescues us and there is no room for anything more. When God calls us, and He does call us every day, we are to leave behind all that is temporary. Go to Him in prayer, in solitude, in joy, in laughter. In one another.

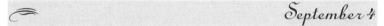

"I tell you, on that night there will be two people in bed; one will be taken, the other left. And there will be two women grinding meal together, one will be taken, the other left."

LUKE 17:34, 35

I love the game of basketball. In my youth, I played every chance I got, and as we all know, the more we practice something the better we become. I practiced free throws (foul shots) until they became second nature to me. I managed a pretty good average, and if chosen to shoot in a game, I rarely missed. (Keep in mind we played half court. Someone had to shoot for the guards.) I was chosen in many clutch situations. Very simply, I practiced, put in time at the gym, and therefore became consistent, so I was chosen.

Jesus tells us today that when the end comes, some will be left behind; not chosen. He wants us to spend time with Him. He wants us to work at being 100 percent. He calls us to put in more time, to practice, and to improve our chances of being chosen in clutch situations and in everyday living. He needs us to spend time in His arena. He wants us to put Him on our schedule of priorities and to be chosen. Be among the chosen.

September 5

"I tell you, he will see to it that justice is done for them speedily. But, when the Son of Man comes, will he find faith on earth?"

LUKE 18:8

I know that anytime I ask my children to do something, they wonder what everyone else has to do. Regardless of whether the request is about doing a chore or going out to eat or to shop, they ask, "Well, what is Beth going to do? Or Nicholas? Or Margaret?" Never fails. What business is it of theirs what other people are doing? They worry about my fairness, no doubt. And maybe they should. But I'm telling them none of these things matter in the big picture. Trust me. It all equals out in the end. Do not worry about everyone else.

Jesus says when it all comes down to it, justice will be served. All will be equal. He's not worried about people getting their just rewards. That will happen. Fairness will reign in the end. But in the end, will He find that we have faith? When He comes again, will He find people on the earth who actually believe in the just One? Today, we are to stop worrying about who is getting what and why and when and how. Have faith.

September 6

"For this reason a man shall leave his father and mother [and be joined to his wife], and the two shall become one flesh. So they are no longer two but one flesh."

MARK 10:7, 8

*W*hen we were young, my mom tried the "new" peanut butter and jelly in one jar. Thinking this would be easier, she proudly placed the jar in the cabinet, or was it in the refrigerator? Maybe that was the problem. We decided it should be kept cold after it was opened because of the jelly, and then the peanut butter was difficult to spread because it was hard. Back to the old way quickly. Let the peanut butter be peanut butter and the jelly be jelly, so when they are put together they are one — perfectly one. The best of both together.

As Jesus speaks to us, He reminds us of the importance of a husband and a wife joining together to become one. They bring out the best of themselves and make a better life. We are called to leave our father and our mother and find our vocation where we will bring the best of ourselves to make this life a little better, to become one with what He has planned for us. Whether we are the thick, smooth peanut butter or the chunky, sweet jelly, we are made to join together with Jesus, with His Church, with one another to become one, to become better. To mesh.

September 7

"Let the children come to me; do not prevent them, for the kingdom of God belongs to such as these. Amen, I say to you, whoever does not accept the kingdom of God like a child will not enter it."

MARK 10:14, 15

I was sitting in Mass several pews in front of a family with an infant who was squalling. I tried to focus on the homily and the presentation of the gifts, but the man a few pews ahead kept glancing back and sneering about the infant. Finally, the baby was taken out and all was calm until right at the consecration, a phone rang. Guess who? Oh my goodness. I couldn't help but think that Jesus was probably much more tolerant of the baby's squalling than the man's cell phone. I don't like to be like this, but I wanted to blow raspberries.

Jesus makes it clear today. Chill out. Relax. Don't take this life too seriously. Keep some innocence. He loves us to be carefree and young and childlike. He loves for us to need Him. We do need Him, and we are never too old to go to Him. Loosen up. Drop the sneer. Go to Him and let Him hold us and love us as we are. As His children.

"If you wish to be perfect, go sell what you have and give to [the] poor and you will have treasure in heaven. Then come, follow me."

MATTHEW 19:21

When I had my first two girls, I saved all their clothes in boxes just in case God sent me more girls. And He did, eight years later and again four years after that. As I proudly removed the clothes I had saved, I noticed the extreme yellow stains on the pastel clothes. I washed with bleach, I spot treated, I tried everything, and even when I was able to remove some of the stains, most of the clothes did not fit during the proper seasons or had elastic that was dry rotted. What a waste of time and effort! If I had given those clothes away years before, they could have been used instead of thrown away.

Jesus calls us to let go of all the material goods of this world and use what we have to help others. He promises us treasure in heaven much greater than we can fathom on this earth. He wants us to let go of the things of this world so that we can follow Him. Leave it all behind today because chances are when we come back to it, it will be useless. Give to those in need.

"Again I say to you, it is easier for a camel to pass through the eye of a needle than for one who is rich to enter the kingdom of God."

MATTHEW 19:24

Every year, I don't fully understand it, but either my children grow or their clothes shrink in the dryer because I am constantly changing the hem on their pants. Even with my reading glasses, it is getting more difficult to put the thread through that tiny slit in the needle to get started. I know, bigger needles, bigger eyes, but then it is more difficult to sew and make it look nice. So, I have grown fond of the "needle threader" with the flexible wire loop on the end that I can slip through the eye of the needle and pull the thread through easily. The cheapest item in the sewing department, and yet I have found it the most helpful.

Jesus tells us that entering His kingdom will not be easy. He never said life would be easy. His way is simple but difficult, especially in today's world. We have to go against the grain. We have to find the tiniest little loop holes, and we have to make conscious efforts. We have to fit into the smallest spaces. We have to work hard at the most difficult tasks. Strive to pass.

September 10

"Amen, I say to you, there is no one who has given up house or brothers or sisters or mother or father or children or lands for my sake and for the sake of the gospel who will not receive a hundred times more now in this present age: houses and brothers and sisters and mothers and children and lands, with persecutions, and eternal life in the age to come."

MARK 10:29, 30

Many Dominican Sisters in our local congregation can tell their conversion story and it sounds close to what Jesus says to us today. They heard the voice of God call them, and they left boyfriends and parents and homes and they traveled to a small piece of land near downtown Nashville to preach and to teach for the sake of the Gospel. From different countries, from other states, from local areas, they drop all they have for Jesus' sake.

Jesus calls us in a similar way perhaps to drop all we have on our agenda. He calls us to leave our house a little earlier and attend Mass. He calls us to skip our plans for lunch and feed someone who we passed on the road begging for a meal. He asks us to give up the time we set aside for ourselves and visit a sick or elderly person or a lonely friend. Receive, for the sake of the Gospel. Receive.

September 11

"[Or] am I not free to do as I wish with my own money? Are you envious because I am generous?"

MATTHEW 20:15

I cannot think of this date without remembering the year 2001 when terrorists flew planes into the World Trade Towers in New York City killing over 2700 people. My mom and two of our coworkers were in Chicago waiting to fly to Italy. I frantically began trying to phone my mom along with the many others who called loved ones attempting to "fly the friendly skies." America is one country who I can definitely say welcomes all. Who could possibly not love us? In their hearts are they envious of our goodness? I know that the devil is envious of our goodness. The devil always tries to destroy those who do good deeds. We fight for other countries' freedoms. We help poor countries, devastated countries, countries that cannot seem to help themselves. God bless America.

Envy is alive and well and flourishing in the hearts and minds of many people. Jesus says do not stop being generous because of the way others treat us. Do not stop giving freely for the sake of other human beings. Envy eats away at the heart, and if we let it in it will tear us apart. Take care of one another. Give when it is the hardest to give. Do not be afraid. Be generous.

September 12

"The cup that I drink, you will drink, and with the baptism with which I am baptized, you will be baptized; but to sit at my right or at my left is not mine to give but is for those for whom it has been prepared."

MARK 10:39, 40

At every large "sit down" dinner party I have ever helped set-up (truthfully not many), there have been place cards to mark where people are to sit. I've worked with the cards and put forth extreme effort to place people where they will be comfortable and have fun. I place people together who have life experiences in common whether business or family related. Everyone at the party is welcome to eat and to drink all that is prepared. I am happy to serve. But please, please, please don't swap the place cards.

Jesus tells us that a place has been prepared for us. He has gone before us, and He has saved us a place. We now must not just be baptized, but we must also share in the cup of salvation. We must attend the banquet and drink the cup, share His life, and follow His lead. We must walk in His footsteps so we can earn the place He has reserved for us. He's not changing around the place cards, but He can invite us to our place at the banquet. Take. Receive.

"Just so, the Son of Man did not come to be served but to serve and to give his life as a ransom for many."

MATTHEW 20:28

While working on a project about the apparitions of Mary, I was led to read about Our Lady of Ransom. When Mary appeared to St. Peter Nolasco she asked him to start the Mercedarian Order devoted to the rescue of Christian captives from the Moors. Priests prayed and gathered the means to "buy back" Christians. Lay monks and knights went into the camps of the Moors and paid them for captives, or, if necessary, traded places with the captives to gain their freedom. I can't help but think of the many men and women today who serve our country and put themselves in harm's way for the safety of my family. Our military, our police officers, and our firefighters all serve and risk their lives for others every day.

Jesus tells us of the unselfishness of those who come to serve and pay the price for others. He came to serve us and to offer His life in place of ours. We now have an open door opportunity to gain Heaven. What an incredible service! May we be grateful to Jesus for His dying love for us, but also grateful to the thousands of men and women who sacrifice every day for our safety. Always be grateful.

"What do you want me to do for you?"

MARK 10:51

One of my favorite television shows from the 1960s is *I Dream of Jeannie*. An astronaut finds a lantern on the beach and rubs it, summoning a 2,000-year-old genie. The show is filled with the genie responding to what she "thinks" her "master" wants her to do. She would pop out of her bottle leaving some smoke behind and ask, "What would you like me to do for you?" Then she'd cross her arms and blink and nod and in an instant it was done. Most requests were misunderstood, and the thirty minutes were filled with undoing Jeannie's mess. The part that made us all laugh was guessing how Jeannie would answer the astronauts, Tony and Roger, and how she would fix things before their boss, Captain Bellows, caught on to the truth.

Jesus asks us a very simple question that requires a straight answer. "What do you want me to do for you?" Wow. Do we wish to be healed? Do we wish to see? Do we wish some blessing for someone else? He wants us to say what we want. We may not get a response immediately or we may. We may not get the answer that we hoped for or we may. He asks us to state our requests. And believe.

September 15

"Have sight; your faith has saved you."

LUKE 18:42

I take sight for granted. Sure of it. I can see to drive, to read, to write, and yet I close my eyes to so many things that need my attention. What will really save me from myself? What will open my eyes to the life that is right in front of me? The man on the street who asks for a handout? My mother who asks to spend time together? My husband or a child who asks for one more thing? My dad who asks me to stop by? Somewhere along the way I have to believe that if I do the right thing, I will then be able to see.

Jesus gives us the gift of sight if we have the faith to really accept His gift. Faith can save us. Faith will save us from ourselves and from all that blinds us from the truth. He does not want us to continue on a blind path. He wants us to open our eyes to the possibilities and the gifts that He offers. He gives us sight. He calls us to bring our life into focus. Have sight.

September 16

"Zacchaeus, come down quickly, for today I must stay at your house."

LUKE 19:5

I have made many climbs in my life to see more clearly. I have climbed Cross Hill in Medjugorje, climbed to the life-size Stations of the Cross in Lourdes, the short, many stairs to Sacra Coeur and the hill at Mont San Michel, all to see something more, something breath-taking, something I may never see again. I have climbed trees, climbed up on shoulders, and climbed ladders for a better view. I have climbed into cars, into trains, onto buses, and onto planes to go and see.

Jesus tells us to come down and see what He has in store for us. Do not worry about trying to get higher in this life. Do not strain to see something more. Do not look for anything more breathtaking than what is right here in front of us. He is here with us. He has come into our house to stay, and we need not do anything more than come down and be with Him. The crowds of this world cannot keep Him from us. We do not need to travel. We do not need to climb. He seeks us out. Come down.

September 17

"Today salvation has come to his house because this man too is a descendent of Abraham. For the Son of Man has come to seek and to save what was lost."

LUKE 19:9, 10

*M*any years ago, about a month after we opened St. Mary's Bookstore at the new location, we suffered a major fire. My mom and I arrived as firemen were leaving after hosing down the last burning embers. When we were allowed to enter, we hunted through the ashes, searching for something, anything, to salvage. Even the few boxes of items we saved smelled of smoke weeks later. The store was considered a total loss.

Jesus brings salvation to all of us. He does not speak of saving who He can because He does not come to salvage, He comes to save. He comes for all of us lost in a world of hate and hardship, of happiness and overabundance, and of poverty and work. He comes for the overachievers as well as the underachievers. He comes for those who follow Him and those who have wandered far away. Jesus comes to seek and to bring salvation to all. Jesus calls us to Himself. Be open to His call. Be aware. Jesus saves.

September 18

"Let her alone. Why do you make trouble for her? She has done a good thing for me."

MARK 14:6

*A*s the mother of four girls and two boys, I must say "Let her alone" at least five times a day. Why is it that our children have to pick on one another? Why is it that they try to get one another in trouble? Even when one of them is doing something good, the others tend to give them a hard way to go. I have to wonder. Is it because they are jealous that they did not think to help me out, or are they just picking on one another? Is it all about getting my attention? If one helps me with dinner, another bellows out that she just wants something. If one puts away the toys in the playroom, the other says it is because she has lost something. For the last time, "let her alone."

Jesus tells us to leave others alone especially when they are trying to do "a good thing." So many times we tend to jump on the bandwagon talking about another person's pious acts or good intentions or holy longing. We question other's motives because their actions tend to strike a chord in us that make us question our own spirituality. Jesus knows our intentions, and He says, "Let her alone." Do something good.

September 19

"The poor you will always have with you, and whenever you wish you can do good to them, but you will not always have me."

MARK 14:7

As I drop off children for school, I pass right by the church on my way to work. Some mornings I can hear Jesus ask, "Do you have the time?" All the good work that I am headed off to do can wait forty-five minutes after I stop in and spend time with the One who loves me unconditionally. I can often feel the pull between the business of Jesus and the time with Jesus, and I know I may not always have this opportunity. Obviously, time spent with Jesus in Mass would help with the business decisions during the day.

Jesus makes it clear that He wants to be our priority. He does not say anything about not tending to others because by helping others we are helping Him. It seems that when we put Him first, all the other needs of the day fall into place. We are called to put Jesus above all else, and in so doing we can see clearly His work that needs to be done. Make time for Him.

September 20

"She has done what she could. She has anticipated anointing my body for burial."

MARK 14:8

*I*n our retail store business, we tend to anticipate the needs of our customers. In the spring we buy for the Christmas Season, and in the fall we buy for the Easter Season. This allows importers to order and receive and ship our merchandise in time for the selling season. Some years we are right on target fulfilling needs, and other years we are a little off. Either way, we can say that we honestly have done what we can do in anticipation of the needs of our customers.

Jesus says "good job" in anticipating the needs of others. When we plan in advance, when we are organized, when we work toward a goal, we can get so much more done. As we look ahead toward our day, our week, and our month, Jesus wants us to anticipate the needs of others and to include those needs in our plans. We can make a difference.

September 21

"I tell you, if they keep silent, the stones will cry out!"

LUKE 19:40

*L*ate in my forties, I happened upon an "open house" at the house where I was raised. I walked in to find the house had just received a contract, but the real estate agent said I was welcome to look around. I could not believe, first, how much smaller everything was than I remember, but also how well I remembered the layout and the rooms. Memories came rushing back to me, and I thought, "Oh, if these walls could speak." Then again, if they could speak, they may be more accurate in their storytelling. I tend to leave out parts that do not work in my favor.

Jesus tells us to share His story. We are commissioned to pass on all that He has passed on to us. We cannot keep His words for ourselves. They are meant for all to hear. Speak about Him. Teach His truth. Otherwise, that "cry out" may tend to leave out the very parts we need to hear. Spread His message.

September 22

"If this day you only knew what makes for peace — but now it is hidden from your eyes."

LUKE 19:42

$\mathcal{M}$any days I feel like peace is hidden in the hecticness of our lives, in our work, in our routine, and in our children. We shake hands for peace, we sign peace, and we pray for peace. We sing about peace and we talk peace, but we absolutely do not know what "makes for peace." The prayer of St. Francis says that to be an instrument of the peace of Christ, we must console, understand, love, give, pardon, and die to self. We must live always thinking of others. I was friends with a priest who seemed to truly live this prayer. He took time with our children as well as the sick at home and in the hospitals. He listened to those who needed to talk, and he gave to those in need. He let the "stuff" that others said or did slide right off his back. He was completely selfless. When you met him eye to eye, he could calm your soul. He brought peace.

Jesus says to seek peace. Seek what makes for peace. Peace is not something we can see, not a sign or a symbol. He knows that true peace is not something easily grasped. He wants us to know that it is so much more. Work for what makes for peace. We are called to be peace to one another, to console another, to hear what is being said, to love unconditionally, to give without expecting in return, to forgive all. Live every day for God.

September 23

"Is it not written: / 'My house shall be called a house of prayer for all peoples'? / But you have made it a den of thieves."

MARK 11:17

$\mathcal{G}$rowing up, our house seemed to have a revolving door. All were welcome, and all came and went freely. All were included, all were fed, and all were allowed to stay as long as they acted appropriately. My sister loves to tell the story when a group of her friends spent the night on the pool room floor and I denied some of them blankets for the night because I thought they were not nice. I was a great judge of character back then. They probably stole my champion title at pool and I was mad. Dang thieves! I should have made them leave.

Jesus speaks to us about inclusion. He welcomes all into His house, and we should follow His example. When someone abuses His invitation, they should be asked to leave, but otherwise, all are welcome. All are welcome to pray, all are fed, and all are allowed to stay. In our house today, in our hearts today, allow others to come in.

Feed those who need to be fed, pray with them, nurture them, and, unless they act inappropriately, allow them a place to continually feel welcome. Include all.

"Therefore I tell you, all that you ask for in prayer, believe that you will receive it and it shall be yours."

MARK 11:24

I know when teaching my child to ride a bike, she could ride well until she started thinking about things too much. She allowed doubt to enter, and she crashed. For weeks she continually fell over or jumped off. The tiniest bit of doubt, and the ride was over for the day. Little by little she came to believe that she could ride a bike. She talked herself into getting on and riding, and she never crashed again. It was quick, and it was done. "I believe I can ride."

Jesus tells us to ask for what we want in prayer and to believe. No hint of doubt. No maybe or probably. No skepticism. Full-blown belief that we will receive. It really is not as easy as it sounds in this world of fear and doubt, but we are called to listen and to believe. Set all else aside today. Ask in prayer. Believe and receive.

"When you stand to pray, forgive anyone against whom you have a grievance, so that your heavenly Father may in turn forgive you your transgressions."

MARK 11:25

I n our Christian bookstore and church goods business, it is difficult to get over people who write us bad checks or steal items or do not pay their account. It is difficult to understand, but it doesn't mean we hold a grudge. We had one person who stole from us, then after going through a recovery program, came by to ask forgiveness. I knew she was stealing. I had to let her go, and I was also moved by her request for forgiveness.

Jesus says not "if" you pray, but "when" you pray forgive anyone with whom you have a problem, any problem. He knows there will be those who ask for forgiveness, and He knows there will be those who will not care one way or the other, and we are told today to forgive them all. No matter what someone else has done and no matter what we do, it is not always for us to understand, but is always for us to forgive. Forgive all.

"Neither shall I tell you by what authority I do these things."

LUKE 20:8

Growing up in a family of ten, we had to ask permission to do and to use anything, or someone would tell. Does Donna know you're using her skates? Does mom know you're at Maureen's house? Does Phillip know you've got his glove? Does Mike know you're playing his records? Well, it was never their business. It was between me and that person, but I said yes regardless, to get people off my back. I don't have to say it, but I do have the authority to use the skates, to go to Maureen's, to use his glove, and to play his records. So back off and mind your own business.

Jesus speaks to us about His authority on earth. He was sent to us, and He was given permission to cure and to preach and to love and to live and to die for us so that others might have life in Him. His message is not for us to question. It is definitely not our business to wonder why or how. It is however our business to believe and to follow and to pass on. Jesus may not reveal every little reason to us, but we are still expected to have faith. Pass along faith.

"Therefore, I say to you, the kingdom of God will be taken away from you and given to a people that will produce its fruit."

MATTHEW 21:43

Athletes hate to be benched. As spectators, we see the disappointment as a pitcher is removed from the mound. We see the anger as a basketball player heads to the bench. We see helmets pulled from heads as football players run for the sidelines. But as spectators, we want to see the results of a good replacement. We want our teams to win. We want the game to progress in our favor. And as we get deeper into the season, we need to see improvements. We want it. The athletes want it. The head coaches want it. And if we do not get the winning results, we want the position taken away and given to someone else; someone to help the team win.

Jesus calls us to listen to His commands. He wants us to be productive in His name, about His kingdom. He does not want to send in replacements, but He will do what He has to do to feed His people. He wants us to spread His Word, to light His lamp, to bring others to Him. He wants us to preach and to teach and to love one another, or He'll just get others to do His work so that all may benefit and all may win. We must do His will or He'll find someone else. Help Him win.

September 28

"Have you not read this scripture passage: / 'The stone that the builders rejected / has become the cornerstone, / by the Lord has this been done, / and it is wonderful in our eyes'?"

MARK 12:10, 11

*M*y first rejections from publishers were difficult. I thought I had fresh ideas that everyone would love and that would sell over and over and over. There were a few who liked the ideas and sent back manuscripts with suggestions, but also with notes that read, "Sorry. Not at this time." There were others who did not respond. With every rejection, there grew within me the sense to learn more and to practice and to read. I cannot yet wallpaper my bathroom with these notices, but I will save them for future possibilities.

Jesus shares with us the importance of reading Scripture and putting it into our lives. Rejection is a part of life. Rejection is important enough to be taught about in the Scriptures. Learning from the Scriptures, learning from rejection will make us stronger. Jesus tells us that it is wonderful when we use these lessons to build ourselves up. Read the Scriptures. Become a cornerstone for Christ.

September 29

"Many are invited, but few are chosen."

MATTHEW 22:14

*A*ny athletic team I have ever tried to play on has only kept those who were the best. When I went to try out for the women's basketball team at Vanderbilt, I was completely unprepared. I had taken time off my freshman year to enjoy college life, and I found myself overweight and under-skilled. The coaches let anyone try to make the team, and I had become one of those. Anyone. I could shoot from anywhere on the court and score if someone could just pull me up and down in a wagon. The coach was nice enough to take me into his office and compliment my abilities but break the news that I was extremely too far "out of shape" to be chosen for the team.

Jesus tells us that all of us are welcome, and all of us are invited to share in His life, but few will be chosen. If we want to be with Him, we have to get our spiritual lives in shape. We are called upon to work diligently and continually, and to accept all that He has invited us to in this life, so that we may be chosen to share in an eternal life with Him. Prepare because we can all "try out" but not everyone will be found fit for the long haul. Get in shape spiritually. Be chosen.

September 30

"Then repay to Caesar what belongs to Caesar and to God what belongs to God."

LUKE 20:25

I complain about paying taxes. Each year my husband goes downtown and fights the increase in our property tax, and each year he gets a little taken off, but not much. Truth is we do have the property. It is probably worth close to what they say. The presidents' faces are right there on the front of the dollar bills, and I should just pay the government what they are owed. And in the overall picture, I do.

Jesus is speaking to us about much more than our taxes and our government. He wants us to give back to the world what belongs to the world, and to God what belongs to God. He wants us to give not just our treasure, but also our time and talent. Discovering our gifts and freely sharing them with others is all He wants us to accomplish in this life. We are asked to fully discover our own gifts. Give something back.

October 1

"You are misled because you do not know the scriptures or the power of God."

MATTHEW 22:29

$\mathcal{M}$any years ago as I rode a train through Italy, a young man came and sat in the seat right next to mine. It didn't take long for him to notice I was riding alone and so began talking to me nonstop. Oh joy! General conversation turned to Scripture quickly. He rattled about science and religion for what seemed like an hour before the train stopped and it was time for me to get off the train and out of the conversation. I didn't care where I landed. I was just glad to get away from the pelting questions about my beliefs.

Jesus stresses the importance of knowing Scripture. He knows how easy it is to be misled by those who want to draw us away from Him. He knows the lengths that others will go to when they start to feel us sway in our beliefs. Jesus wants us to be strong in our faith. He wants us to listen to the Scriptures and to know the saving power of God. He wants us to know truth. Do not be misled.

October 2

"My food is to do the will of the one who sent me and to finish his work. Do you not say, 'In four months the harvest will be here'? I tell you, look up and see the fields ripe for the harvest."

JOHN 4:34, 35

$\mathcal{I}$ am reminded of a picture I've seen many times entitled "The Gleaners." The artist portrays three women in a field picking up the last scraps of wheat after the harvest. Sometimes don't you feel like that is what we're on earth to do; pick up the pieces, clean up the mess, follow up, finish the job? No matter our call in life, we often find ourselves in these circumstances. Whether in business or at home with our families or in our communities, we find ourselves taking care until the last bit of work is complete. Gleaners. Critics view this famous painting as a contrast of power and poverty, but I see that although the man in the background stands with stacks of wheat from the harvest, until the last little grains are saved and all are gathered together, the job is not finished.

Jesus calls us to the harvest. Our fields, our homes, our neighborhoods, and our businesses are bursting with the need to be gathered in, to be brought together. And He promises that if we do this work, His Father's will, we will have all we need. His work will sustain us. We will be fed, and we will be satisfied. But we must go out, we must do the hard work, we must save even the smallest grains, those that others may never notice. The fields are ripe. The harvest is now.

"The Lord our God is Lord alone! You shall love the Lord your God with all your heart, with all your soul, with all your mind, and with all your strength."

MARK 12:29, 30

The first time I felt true love, I could not think of anything else. I thought about him all day while we were apart. We wrote letters back and forth as he finished college, and I couldn't wait for the phone to ring so I could hear his voice. My heart would race when I knew he was coming home for the weekend. After we married, I would hop the stairs to our apartment two by two to reach him faster so I could see his face. Although we work together at the store and at home, I still look forward to spending time with him.

Jesus speaks to us about wanting all the love we can possibly give. He wants us to get excited about sitting with Him. He wants us to "hop two steps at a time" to go to Mass. He wants us to rejoice in the time we have together. He wants us to think about Him all through our day. With all our heart, with all our soul, and with all our strength, may we love our God. Love Him.

"'You shall love your neighbor as yourself!' There is no other commandment greater than these."

MARK 12:31

I know why Jesus has asked me to love my neighbor in particular and not just people in general. Neighbors are right here every day. They are next to us at the beginning when all is well, and they are still there when our children pick their flowers to bring us a surprise or when our customers park in their parking spaces. They are right there when our daughters have friends with loud trucks to drive them home at midnight or when the delivery trucks take up the entire entrance to the parking lot. They are right there when they throw debris from their yard to our yard or their workers fill our dumpsters with their garbage.

Jesus tells us that our neighbor is anyone we come in contact with or simply pass by during the day. He knows how difficult basic relationships are on this earth. He experienced quite a few Himself, but He wants us to love one another despite the challenges; especially the ones right next door who we come into contact with day in and day out. Love your neighbor anyway.

October 5

"Beware of the scribes, who like to go around in long robes and accept greetings in the marketplaces, seats of honor in synagogues, and places of honor at banquets."

MARK 12:38, 39

We have a few people from what I refer to as "made-up" churches come into our bookstore and church supply business and buy many different vestments. They purchase big crosses to wear around their necks and large rings for their fingers. The brighter the colors, the more gold and bold, the better they like them. I don't mean to judge, but the louder they are and the longer the titles before their names, the more skeptical I become about their "business."

Jesus wants us to pay attention to the people around us in this world so that we are not led astray. His world is not about power and position. His world is not about looks. He speaks simply and clearly about love. Jesus calls us to notice the world around us and not to allow ourselves to be sucked into the "things" of this place. He says beware.

October 6

"I tell you truly, this poor widow put in more than all the rest; for those others have made offerings from their surplus wealth, but she, from her poverty, has offered her whole livelihood."

LUKE 21:3, 4

On a college trip with my sister and her friends, we went to Mass with one of the guys on Sunday. I remember that the church was small and open and quite airy, very different from anything we had ever seen. Of course, the Mass, as it is all over the world, was the same, but this one seemed quicker. As the basket was passed I reached in my pocket to pull out a few dollars, leaving plenty for the rest of my trip. I watched as the guy who had come with us pulled out his wallet, gathered every bill, and dropped it into the basket. I'll never forget. Every bill!

Jesus tells us that He does not want our leftovers. He does not want what we have at the end of the day, when we get home from work, or what we have after cooking and cleaning and taking care of children. He wants us as we work, as we cook, as we clean, as we give, as we take. He wants our entire life. He wants us to empty ourselves. Jesus wants our all.

October 7

"All that you see here — the days will come when there will not be left a stone upon another stone that will not be thrown down."

LUKE 21:6

*C*hange of any type can be difficult. I have seen our church and our school from their beginnings change as they have needed due to the growing number of Catholic families they have had to accommodate. Disagreement over changes can make people do and say things completely out of character. One day I was in my car in the school parking lot, and a young mom approached me and accused me of "siding" with the "renovation team" because I "needed" the business for our store. It's brick and mortar!

Jesus calls us to put aside the material world. What we build up in one another is what will matter in the long haul. He doesn't care what the bricks look like or where the statues are placed, but He does care how we treat one another. Jesus tells us that all will be gone someday. Except for us.

October 8

"But the one who perseveres to the end will be saved. And this gospel of the kingdom will be preached throughout the world as a witness to all nations, and then the end will come."

MATTHEW 24:13, 14

I am terrible about not finishing one project before I start another. I get tired of the same things over and over, so I start something new and put many things on "back burners." Painting is one of my favorite projects because I love freshly painted rooms. They make me feel like I have a new home or at least certain areas are new. But I love to roll and hate to trim, so the trim gets put off and put off, until the project is no longer satisfying.

Jesus tells us to persevere in the tasks He calls us to do so that we can be saved. He does not want us just to do the wide open easy parts. He wants us to perform the tedious little intricate parts as well, and He wants us to complete the tasks. Jesus calls us to witness to the world. Persevere in His name.

October 9

"See that no one deceives you."

MARK 13:5

*I*n our family we are very specific about rules. Every child knows not to ask me about inviting a friend over in front of the friend or their mom. Every child knows they do not get in a neighbor's car for a ride home when they can walk just fine. Every child knows I am not bringing something to a friend's house if they inadvertently left it up in their room. Their hand-held anythings are to be off the floor and in a case or in their hands. However, it never fails that I get this: "But Mom, so and so said...." "But Mom, they told us...." "But Mom...." Their responsibility is to know the rules so that they are not tricked into believing that I will suddenly change my ways.

Jesus calls us to have responsibility. He has given us all we need, and He will back us up with His Spirit. We must in turn know our faith and be strong in our beliefs so that we are not deceived. No "if this" or "but that." Jesus wants us to know. See to it. He is truth. There is no one else.

October 10

"Nation will rise against nation and kingdom against kingdom. There will be earthquakes from place to place and there will be famines. These are the beginnings of the labor pains."

MARK 13:8

*W*ith the birth of each of my children, I disliked more and more getting an epidural. I realize that I just felt pressure in my back, but I just didn't care for it much. So with the last child, as the doctor met me for delivery, I asked if I could try having this baby natural. He had no problem since I had given birth five times previously, but he warned me that there was no going back. Well! I had no idea. Labor pains are, shall we just say, intense. Indescribably intense. But I did well and Julia did well and the doctor and the nurse were pleased. Of course, not as pleased as if it had been planned, but pleased.

Jesus warns us of some trials in this world. And for all who think the beginnings of the labor pains are rough, you cannot imagine. This is the world. Unfortunately, we were never told any of this would be easy, and with each experience of a disaster we realize that there must be something better. We could even question at times if this is what hell would be like for some of these people. Jesus wants us to cling to Him in good times and in bad. And there will be bad.

October 11

"But the gospel must first be preached to all nations."

MARK 13:10

"First things first" my mom would always say to us kids, which usually meant we needed to do projects her way or the day would be a disaster. But she was normally correct. First we make a list of everything we need. Then we go to the grocery store, unload groceries, clean counters, turn on oven, and so on. I can't tell you how many times after I moved away from her that I started a project and had to stop halfway through and run to the store because I didn't make a list. First things first.

Jesus calls us to put things in order. The Gospel is to be preached to everyone. For us, it starts in our family and our community at church and at work and in our neighborhood. We must first all be on the same page and know what is expected and know the message of the Gospel. Jesus tells us to first preach, by word and by example. Everything in proper order.

October 12

"But say whatever will be given to you at that hour. For it will not be you who are speaking but the holy Spirit."

MARK 13:11

One day in our bookstore, I was talking with a guy about his desire to become Catholic because "we" have the opportunity, the gift, to receive Jesus Christ in the Eucharist every day. As I listened and shared, I consciously asked the Holy Spirit to guide my words. I do not know enough to be technical with anyone about religion. I'm constantly reading and constantly learning, and I know why I believe what I believe, but to pass that on in "catechism" terms is difficult for me. So, I say a prayer. In this instance, I really couldn't tell you what was said, but the Spirit was definitely present between us.

Jesus allows us to let go of our fears. He allows us to relax and let the Holy Spirit work through us. All day and every day we are to let go of worry and let the Spirit speak. He wants us to be examples, to teach and to preach and to spread the Good News. We will encounter those who know more, those who want to know more, and those who will oppose us, and He will take over. Whatever He gives us at that hour is all we will need. Let the Spirit speak.

October 13

"Amen, amen, I say to you, you will see the sky opened and the angels of God ascending and descending on the Son of Man."

JOHN 1:51

We stand in complete awe and wonder at the sight of the sun slowly dropping into the ocean with tints of orange and red we have never seen. We stand with jaw dropped and call others to come see the colors of the rainbow streaked across the sky after a spring shower. We slow down our drive approaching a mountain range in autumn amazed at the different shades of color in each tree; the uniqueness of every peak; the majesty of the painting. Each year I drive through the Smokey Mountains to attend a retreat in Maggie Valley, North Carolina. It is always October. The leaves are turning and the mountains are filled with a multi-color majesty. I am constantly stunned.

Jesus calls us to open our eyes to what He can do. He tells us that we will see amazing things if we stick with Him day in and day out. Skies opening, angels ascending and descending. He is our key to all the wonders of earth and of heaven. There are so many great things He can lead us through; He can show us, if we abandon ourselves to Him. What Jesus has in store for those who follow Him is greater than a sunset or a rainbow or the turning leaves of trees. May we walk with eyes wide open. Be prepared to be amazed.

October 14

"When their buds burst open, you see for yourselves and know that summer is now near; in the same way, when you see these things happening, know that the kingdom of God is near."

LUKE 21:30, 31

Bl. Pope John Paul II spoke of a new springtime in the Church. There is much work to do in spring as there is much to do in our Church. We are called to evangelize so that we can witness "newness," fresh buds that burst open. Being around Catholics who have come back to the Church or "new" Catholics, I witness firsthand the enthusiasm and the work that they want to do to go tell everyone the Good News — to share what they have found or have rediscovered. This springtime, this "newness," this evangelization, pushes us closer to building the kingdom.

Jesus calls us to pay attention to the work at hand. This is a new time for the Church. We see buds about to bloom and understand that summer is close. We are asked to witness "newness." We are asked to work for the kingdom of God. Be witnesses for Christ.

October 15

"Heaven and earth will pass away, but my words will not pass away."

MATTHEW 24:35

I cannot tell you how often I get asked for Bibles with the feature "Christ's words in red." Needless to explain, the wording throughout the book is in black except for the words of Jesus, which are in red. There are actually not many Catholic translations that have His words in red. I guess it's a publishing preference, not a translation preference, but I personally like the feature. After all, His words are truth and life.

Jesus tells us that His words are everlasting. They will not pass away. They will not go bad. His words are timeless, and His words are forever. Each and every day we are to listen to and heed the words of Jesus. All of the physical aspects of the world will pass. Not His words.

"It is like a man traveling abroad. He leaves home and places his servants in charge, each with his work, and orders the gatekeeper to be on watch."

MARK 13:34

When my younger brothers were teenagers, the minute my parents would leave town they would start inviting friends over to our house. At the time, I was the oldest at home, and I would be around in case "things" got out of hand. We knew stories of young kids who just invite a "few" people over and soon police have to come and send everyone home because of complaints by neighbors. I wanted no police. I wanted no complaints. I was generally there to keep watch and to have fun. Their friends were a little intimidated by me for the most part.

Jesus places us in charge. We each have some assigned work, which we must figure out through the guidance of the Holy Spirit. We each have a gatekeeper to be on watch so we are never alone in our tasks. We have set out on a journey, and we are awaiting the time when we can come home. We are called to the work, and we are in charge. Today walk His walk. Be on watch. Travel the call.

"Beware that your hearts do not become drowsy from carousing and drunkenness and the anxieties of daily life, and that that catch you by surprise like a trap."

LUKE 21:34, 35

The anxieties of daily life can certainly sometimes seem overwhelming. I fill my day with unreasonable amounts of tasks. I wake early enough to read, to write, and to pray in silence. I wake my children and help them get breakfast. I pack lunches and help the girls with their hair. I take them to school and then go into work at the bookstore. I pay bills, talk with salespeople, take orders, wait on customers as I relieve employees for lunch. I try to be home by three o'clock when the children come home from school unless it's raining — then I pick them up. I help get snacks and prepare for dinner. We do homework between running back and forth to basketball practices. We eat, finish homework, take showers, and prepare for bed. I spend about thirty minutes or so talking with my husband before I fall asleep in the chair. This does not even include dentist and doctor visits, teacher conferences, shooting television commercials, or buying trips to Chicago and Atlanta.

Jesus shakes us from our sleep. He awakes us from our drowsiness, and He calms our anxieties of daily life. He wants us to live wide-eyed and ready so that nothing or no one can trap us and catch us unaware. Jesus wants us alert.

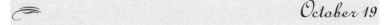

October 18

"Be vigilant at all times and pray that you have the strength to escape the tribulations that are imminent and to stand before the Son of Man."

LUKE 21:36

*I*mminent tribulations. During bad economic times, we witness the failure of many small businesses. They are forced to close because the customers who have always supported their mission have themselves been forced to watch spending. Larger companies who can afford to buy in large quantities offer better prices during these times because more people are suddenly flocking to their "deals." All we as small business owners can do is to be vigilant and pray that our companies have the strength to withstand the big guys during these times. We cut back and work harder when we recognize the imminent tribulations.

Jesus calls us to be on watch. We pray for the strength to escape these tribulations. We know that trials in life will occur, and the way we handle them will be an example to the people around us. May we be examples of His strength and His love as we pray to escape these tough times. Be ready, stand watch. Pray every day.

October 19

"And he will separate them from one another, as a shepherd separates the sheep from the goats."

MATTHEW 25:32

*M*any of us know friends who tend to lead us away from our goals or our responsibilities. "Ahhh, come on. You don't need to go to work." "Come on, stay out a little bit longer." "Climb up, it's safe." "Come over, no one's home." "Your spouse won't mind." "Your parents won't care." "Your friends will understand." I occasionally have young girls at work who do so much better if they stay on separate floors at our bookstore. I have children who just should not sit next to each other in church. I know parents who feed off each other to blow situations out of proportion.

Jesus tells us that He wants to separate us from those who may lead us astray. He knows this world is full of trouble-makers. He knows how our weaknesses tend to misguide us. He is our Shepherd, and He is who we are to follow. Jesus is among us. He protects. He separates.

October 20

"Amen, I say to you, whatever you did for one of these least brothers of mine, you did for me."

MATTHEW 25:40

When we were growing up, my mom had hung a poster in our basement of a young boy with a slightly larger boy on his back. Under the picture was the caption, "He's not heavy, he's my brother." I believe it was the motto used by Fr. Flanagan, the founder of Boys Town. I find it funny that I remember all the posters and holy cards and "sayings" my mom posted around our house. Sometimes the old saying is true, "a picture is worth a thousand words." My mom also knew the importance of getting her words and lessons through to us, thus causing a trickle effect to others.

Jesus calls us to take care of one another as if we were taking care of Him. Working for the least, feeding, serving, loving, and caring for others, is like working for Him. As we have seen it done, so we do, and so on and so on and so on. Jesus calls us to do for those who cannot do for themselves. Work for Jesus.

October 21

"Amen, amen, I say to you, unless a grain of wheat falls to the ground and dies, it remains just a grain of wheat; but if it dies, it produces much fruit."

JOHN 12:24

Oftentimes, artists become more popular after they die. They may try their entire lives to be famous, and yet their work may only produce fortunes after they are gone. Saints on the other hand are often trying to live simple lives, and because of their holiness tend to attract flocks of people who wish to see them and to touch them and to be around them. Their life is as productive when they are alive as it is when they are gone. Bl. Mother Teresa of Calcutta is a wonderful example of someone who never worked for the popularity of herself but for the popularity of those she served so that they could continue to be served by others.

Jesus calls us to die to ourselves. He wants us to forget about all our own wants and needs and to focus on others so that the work that needs done on this earth can be done. When we die to this life, we allow God's love to grow. When we work for God, and not for ourselves, we produce fruit. Be productive.

October 22

"Whoever loves his life loses it, and whoever hates his life in this world will preserve it for eternal life."

JOHN 12:25

I have, more than once, heard my children use the phrase, "I hate my life." Of much concern to their mother, I always delve into what's going on with them and do they need help or a shoulder or an ear. However, it is generally about a friendship or a game or clothes or an event they can't go to or something else that will pass in about an hour. Life is just not fair, and if it were it wouldn't be of this world. We were not put in this world to love this life. We were put here to work and to live and to love for something more. So, go ahead and "hate your life," but use it to an advantage to gain something more.

Jesus makes His feeling about this world clear. This is nothing. Let it go. Live in it, make the best of it, and use it by doing everything we can for others so we can gain eternal life. Save the real living for the next place. There's so much more.

October 23

"Whoever serves me must follow me, and where I am, there also will my servant be. The Father will honor whoever serves me."

JOHN 12:26

I sat at a luncheon held by the Catholic Book Club and listened to two sisters from the Daughters of Charity speak about their work. They shared the idea that St. Vincent believed that in service work, one often had to get the job done any way possible. Sister told a story where she found furniture for a family of six and arranged one weekend for a man with his truck to meet and take the goods to the family. Sister and one of the priests who often helps her went to the house, but the man never showed. Father left and returned with a rowboat strapped to the trunk of his car. After several trips, the furniture was transferred, and the family served. Creative service.

Jesus speaks to us of the importance of following and of serving Him. As we serve those around us each day, our children, our spouses, our coworkers, our neighbors, and strangers we meet, we serve Jesus Himself. We follow His lead as we serve one another. Sometimes it may seem a natural reaction, but at the end of the day, when all are served, His work is honored. Serve Jesus; serve others.

October 24

"But it was for this purpose that I came to this hour. Father, glorify your name."

JOHN 12:27, 28

I will never forget the day, the hour, the moment when an editor from my first publisher called me at our bookstore and told me they wanted to publish my prayer book for mothers. My mom was with me, and we were so excited we both had tears in our eyes, and I was thinking, "For this purpose I have worked and I have waited." All the hard work of putting together a book and sending copies to different publishers and reviewing comments and making changes had paid off. All the time I spent in the wee hours of the night nursing a baby with one arm while writing with the opposite one. I wrote prayers not just for the one in my arms but for those still in their beds and for the life they had ahead of them.

Jesus speaks to us of our purpose. His words, His life teach us that in each moment of every day, there is something that fulfills God's plan. Jesus' hour saved us. He opened the gates of Heaven and defeated death forever. He wants us to serve our purpose. What is in your hour?

"This voice did not come for my sake but for yours."

JOHN 12:30

Most of my life I have heard my mom say, "I'm not just talking to hear myself talk." I was always in my own world with my own agenda. I really did not want to listen to what my parents had to say, and now, as a parent, I know exactly how they felt. I must have told my children a million times not to throw things in the house, and yet I have broken lamps and dents in walls and knocked over pictures. They seem shocked every time something happens even though I've given them a list of possible mishaps with every request. I say things because I want my children and my coworkers to benefit from my years of mistakes, not just to hear myself talk.

Jesus tells us that the words we hear, His messages, are sent to us for our sakes. God does not speak to save His Son. All that is said is for our benefit. He has the answers that can make life so much better, and His words put eternal life within our reach. Jesus had His working papers. He knew what was going on. We are the ones who need to listen and to obey. Hear His voice.

"The light will be among you only a little while. Walk while you have the light, so that darkness may not overcome you. Whoever walks in the dark does not know where he is going."

JOHN 12:35

The older I get, it seems, the more difficult it is to drive in the dark. Each Spring Break, as I drove my children the 870 miles from Nashville, Tennessee, to Naples, Florida, I began my trip before the sun rose. I was always tired for the first couple of hours, but somehow, knowing that the sun was soon to brighten my drive, I could persist. However, if I overslept that morning or couldn't get the children in the car and had to leave as the sun was already rising, I knew the last hours would be grueling. And they were. Once darkness arrived, everything fell apart, and little details became more complicating. I was tired and vulnerable and overcome with the idea of sleep. One hundred miles in the dark seemed like an eternity.

Jesus wants us to walk in the light so that we can see clearly where we are going. With Jesus, there is no chance of losing our way in darkness. There are fewer complications, and we are not wandering, lost in our lives. Jesus calls us to continually walk in the light. Walk while it's light.

"While you have the light, believe in the light, so that you may become children of the light."

JOHN 12:36

I was fortunate to attend a Catholic grade school and high school. I learned about the Catholic faith for twelve straight years from my teachers at school, and what I learned I believe because my parents reiterated those same teachings in our home. We were expected not just to learn about faith, but to put faith into action. We went to Church on Sundays as a family, we blessed our meals together, we made regular visits to the Chapel, and we helped out in the community. Our school and our home taught us about faith and faith in action so that we could live in the light and become children of God.

Jesus reminds us of the importance of connecting the pieces of our Faith. We can hear about faith and read about faith and witness faith, but we also need to believe and to walk in the light of faith to be His children. We have Him in our midst and, especially with our busy lives, we must believe in Him and carry His light to all we encounter so that darkness does not overpower us. Become children of the light.

"Whoever believes in me believes not only in me but also in the one who sent me, and whoever sees me sees the one who sent me."

JOHN 12:44, 45

E very now and then, I feel that God sends an incident to see my response. One very cold winter day, a regular street guy wandered into our bookstore. We were packed with customers, and I caught sight of him and told him he was welcome but to stay near the front so he didn't drag his wet boots all over the store. He said he'd just wait until his hands warmed. I was waiting on a young couple and caught out of the corner of my eye that the street guy had moved toward the door and finally left. As I finished with the couple, I looked up and noticed that the boy turned and went out our door, so I rang up the sale for the girl. I could see out the front window, and I watched the boy take off his gloves and put them on the street guy's hands.

Jesus wants us to see and to believe that we are sent. We believe in the Father and we believe that He sent His Son, and now we are sent for one another. See and believe, and go out so that others will see and believe. Go where God sends you.

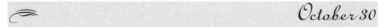

October 29

"And I know that his commandment is eternal life. So what I say, I say as the Father told me."

JOHN 12:50

I used to love to watch certain commentators on the television ad lib when an odd situation occurred or an unusual question was asked by a guest. I would think how smart they were to wiggle their way through with all the right answers. Well, that is , until I watched a movie that burst my bubble. In the movie, the woman commentator wore an earpiece and knew absolutely nothing about certain topics or guests but came through like a charm because someone in a back office was telling her what to say. As she moved farther in her career, she always had to drag a person along with her for all the right answers.

Jesus tells us that He is repeating words directly from His Father. We are fortunate because it's all good news. He's repeating the words of eternal life. He gives us the words of salvation. Jesus calls us to believe in what is to come because the words are from the One with all the right answers. We don't even have to drag Him along. This One wants to be with us and stays forever close. God's words reveal Eternal Life.

October 30

"Go into the city and a man will meet you, carrying a jar of water. Follow him."

MARK 14:13

*B*lind trust. My son and I were at our bookstore late one night, and as we left the parking lot, a young boy running down the street stopped at the car and asked me to roll down the window. "I can hear you just fine." "I don't want money." "Okay." "I missed my bus and need a ride." He was wearing a Wendy's uniform, so I asked my son and he agreed to let him in the car. What a great kid! He and my son talked the entire ride between him saying "turn here," "turn there," "a little farther," and "thank you." I wasn't sure who was more trusting and who was leading who, but he led and I followed and together we got him to the next bus ride toward home. Just to note, my son and I did have the discussion about not picking up strangers.

Jesus speaks to us about an encounter. He instructs us. We are to meet someone, and during a normal day this could be possible. We may lead or we may follow, but most importantly we are to go and we are to have an encounter. The man we follow will certainly be Jesus. Encounter Jesus.

October 31

"Then he will show you a large upper room furnished and ready. Make the preparations for us there."

MARK 14:15

*R*iding the Eurail from Brussels to Brugge, I wondered how I would ever find the vestment company that we had been buying from through our bookstore and church supply company. At the train station, I was looking around for some sort of information area when a man approached me and asked if I needed help. I showed him a business card, and he said he could take me. He offered me a place to stay. In his Volkswagon, my feet straddled the hole in the floor board during the ride. He took me to his home across from his bar and showed me my room, fully furnished with French doors that opened to the canal.

Jesus takes us to the upper room of our hearts. The space is ready. The chamber is open and empty, waiting. We are to consciously go there and prepare for Him to meet us, to fill us so that we can in turn go and do the same. The road that leads us to this place could be long and questionable. There may be chances to take. There may be unknowns. But Jesus meets us. All will be well.

"Do you realize what I have done for you?"

JOHN 13:12

$\mathfrak{M}$y parents have eight children. We all had the privilege of attending Catholic grade school and high school. I did not realize at the time all the sacrifices they made to send us to school. I did not realize what the schools had to offer and how lucky we were to be there until I was out in the real world. We had to get jobs as soon as we were able and we had to pay for many of our own ridiculous wants, but never our basic needs. I did not realize what they had done until I had to do it for myself. I did not realize the time constraints, the money constraints or the energy constraints. I did not realize until I walked in their shoes.

Jesus asks us if we realize what He has done. He wants us to understand His sacrifice. He wants us to know so that we can in turn do, so that we can in turn sacrifice, so that we can in turn walk in His shoes. He does not expect us to do all we do to perfection, but He does want us to realize what can be done. He wants us to open our eyes to the realization of all He has done for us. Appreciate today.

"If I, therefore, the master and teacher, have washed your feet, you ought to wash one another's feet."

JOHN 13:14

$\mathfrak{W}$hen my brother Phillip was in about the seventh grade, he was chosen to have his feet washed at the Mass on Holy Thursday. It was the 70s. We had no odor eaters. We had no foot deodorizers. He did normally have holes in his socks and his socks were usually rather smelly. All I could picture was the priest falling right over the minute he had to bend down and encounter those feet. My mom was way ahead of the possible disaster. New socks and clean shoes awaited Phillip's feet after an extensive bath. Of course, the entire family attended the Mass which, much to my surprise, went smooth as silk. I was hoping for at least a clearing of a throat or a reach toward a nose. But no, feet were washed and service performed and Phillip was proud to be a part of the entire evening.

Jesus calls us to wash feet. He wants us to care for one another regardless of our faults. There are no excuses for today. Clean or dirty, friend or foe, morning or night, Jesus wants us to serve. Today and whenever the opportunity arises, wash feet. With love.

"I have given you a model to follow, so that as I have done for you, you should also do."

JOHN 13:15

One of the things in life that the Dortch family prides itself on is not needing to read instructions before we put anything together. Given a picture or an idea, we can pretty much mimic how an item should look. Besides, part of the fun is in the challenge. Sometimes we may have a few parts left over, some nuts and some bolts or some screws, but the item itself always seems just fine. Occasionally, a family member will have instructions in their hands and someone will blurt out, appalled, "Oh my gosh, you aren't going to read the instructions are you?"

Jesus tells us to live our lives by the model He has given. I find it extremely important to continually place my children around people who model Christ. Life could be so much easier if we were all on the same page of instructions, using the same examples, following the same picture so as to build the same image or shall we say to build up the Kingdom of God together. The Word reminds us that we are called to follow the model given, to work together. Do as Jesus has done.

"From now on I am telling you before it happens, so that when it happens you may believe that I AM."

JOHN 13:19

My parents always seemed to know well in advance when something was going to happen. "If you keep going outside barefoot, you're going to step on a bee." Stung. "If you throw that ball in the house, you're going to break something." Crash. "If you watch that movie, you're going to have bad dreams." Petrified. "If you don't invite the entire class, someone's going to get hurt." Jealousy. "If you eat all the candy, you're going to get sick." Stomachache. "If you talk back, you're going to get in trouble." Detention. "If you don't study, you're going to be sorry." Fail. Parents always seem to know everything before it happens and that's why they are the parents.

Jesus gives us a "heads up." He knows everything before it's going to happen so He wants us to listen to Him. He wants us to open our minds and our hearts and to use our free will to choose to hear His voice, so that when events occur we will know Him and believe. We need to recognize Him so that when He does try to tell us or warn us or give us a "heads up," we believe and heed. Listen to the Lord.

November 5

"I have eagerly desired to eat this Passover with you before I suffer."
LUKE 22:15

We love to gather for meals. The table is the one place where we get a chance to find out all together what is going on in one another's lives. When we gather at my mother's or my sister's or my sister-in-law's house for Thanksgiving and Christmas dinner, the time is spent learning more about one another and laughing and sharing stories. Our lives are always good at the table. A good meal seems to bring out the best in all of us. Differences, if any, are left at the door. We share the meal, and we also share a common Christian life. One gathering. One table. One God.

Jesus eagerly desires us to join Him at the table. He calls us to come and share a meal with Him. At His table, we are one. We leave our differences at the door. We share in His life. We share in His story and our lives are made better as we gather. We are called to come and to eat with Him. Share His meal.

November 6

"Take this and share it among yourselves; for I tell you [that] from this time on I shall not drink of the fruit of the vine until the kingdom of God comes."
LUKE 22:17, 18

I gather occasionally with a group of high school friends for what we call "supper club." Each of us brings a dish of some sort, nothing planned, and we share salads and casseroles and pastas and desserts. Somehow there are rarely duplicates and plenty of variety.

We share a meal, we share pictures of our children and stories of our families or our businesses, and we share a common bond of love. We leave one another with the promise that soon we will come together again to share a meal and to take time with one another.

Jesus offers us a gift to share among ourselves. He gives the gift of Himself, and there is no duplicate. With Him there is plenty of variety, plenty of challenges and differences, but He wants us to share His life and His gift with all we meet. We share this meal and we take time, and together we have a common bond of love. Take and share.

November 7

"This is my body, which will be given for you; do this in memory of me."
LUKE 22:19

For years after I started working at our Catholic bookstore, one of the priests at the Cathedral would come to the store during the summer and remind my mom to "keep an eye out" for Christmas gifts for his fellow priests. Each Christmas, Fr. Fleming hosted a dinner for the priests of the Diocese. Each year my mom would find unique gifts within Fr. Fleming's budget and wrap them in Christmas colors he had approved. After Fr. Fleming died of cancer in July, 1999, the Cathedral continued to host in his memory the Fr. Fleming dinner. The Cathedral parish hall was rebuilt and renamed the "Fleming Center." However, we remember Fr. Fleming not because of the event or the building, but because of the impact he made on the diocese as a man who loved unconditionally and who gave faithfully.

Jesus calls us to imitate what He did at the Last Supper in His memory. He wants us to remember how much He loves us and to take Him out to all the world and to spread that same love to one another. Jesus offers Himself, and we remember not because of the building we stand in, but because of the impact of the man who loves us unconditionally and followed His Father's will faithfully. Give faithfully.

November 8

"Amen, I say to you, one of you will betray me, one who is eating with me."
MARK 14:18

One of my favorite songs growing up was "Nuttin' for Christmas." I guess I felt like it was possibly all about me. "I'm getting

Nuttin' for Christmas, Mommy and daddy are mad, I'm gettin' nuttin' for Christmas, 'cause I ain't been nuttin' but bad. I did a dance on mommy's plants, Climbed a tree and tore my pants, Filled the sugar bowl with ants, Somebody snitched on me." Just take a look around the dinner table. As I sat many nights and ate dinner with my family after spending the day in my room grounded, I wondered which sibling told mom and got me in trouble.

Jesus reminds us that it is not easy to be His follower. He knows that people are jealous of His great love for us. He knows that others will betray us if we follow Him. He knows the one who betrays, and yet He still allows him to eat with Him. Not everyone will like us. Many will be jealous, some will be angry, and some will just be mean, but we must stick to our faith. We must work through our feelings and stay close to Him who can save us. We may not be gettin' nuttin' if we do not remain at the table. Despite what others say.

November 9

"This is how all will know that you are my disciples, if you have love for one another."

JOHN 13:35

My sister Jeanne's children really love one another. They each have their own strengths. They are different, and yet in many ways similar. They each seem to use their talents to the fullest. They admire one another or at least from where I stand that's how it comes across. They love to be around each other either playing games or telling stories, but always laughing and having a great time. Their love spills over to their friends and to the rest of the family. A perfect stranger would know they belong together after being around them only a short time.

Jesus calls us to be recognized because of our love for one another. Others will notice us as His followers if we have love. The way we care for our family and friends, the way we love others who we encounter each day, is the way we are perceived. People judge us by our actions or our lack of action. Love one another. Be His disciple.

"The kings of the Gentiles lord it over them and those in authority over them are addressed as 'Benefactors'; but among you it shall not be so. Rather, let the greatest among you be as the youngest, and the leader as the servant."

LUKE 22:25, 26

When my mother first bought St. Mary's Bookstore, the cash register was an old lever pull style, probably purchased when the store first opened in 1939. When we moved the store, I couldn't wait to change to computers from cash registers and keep track of inventory and sales. I was excited to teach the ladies how to use the computers. They, however, were more interested in waiting on customers and gift wrapping and finding boxes and chatting. I thought the computers were the greatest upgrade for the store, but the ladies continued to prefer the "hands-on" method.

Jesus calls us to be leaders by serving others. There are so many opportunities today that allow us to sit at our desks or on our phones and conduct every bit of our lives, and the more we learn the more we need to be physically present. But Jesus says that He needs leaders who are willing to serve. He needs us to be "hands-on." He knows the efficiency of technology, but He also knows the importance of human contact. He wants us to be leaders of service. Be present to one another.

"For who is greater: the one seated at table or the one who serves? Is it not the one seated at table? I am among you as the one who serves."

LUKE 22:27

When we gather as a family, my mother tends to stay around the kitchen. Regardless of how much others bring for the meal or want to help, she seems to need to add her personal touch, and believe me, we love her personal touch. She makes sure that everyone eats and gets plenty of second helpings. I have always noticed that she rarely eats an entire meal between getting up and down making sure all are satisfied, because to her we are all just great. She loves to love us, to care for us and to serve us.

Jesus wants to know if we think that being served or serving makes a person greater. In our youth, we may think that the one who sits in the special chair and gets catered to is the greatest. Who wouldn't want to be king or queen? Who wouldn't want special treatment? And who usually gets special treatment is the chief, the head, the one who reigns, the greatest. Don't we feel better when we are being waited on and cared for? Or do we? Truthfully, Jesus wants to know what makes us better. Jesus says that He chooses to serve. In His eyes, in His experience, in His heart, the one who serves is greater. Be the one who serves.

November 12

"It is you who have stood by me in my trials; and I confer a kingdom on you, just as my Father has conferred one on me, that you may eat and drink at my table in my kingdom; and you will sit on thrones judging the twelve tribes of Israel."

LUKE 22:28–30

Oftentimes when people are going through the toughest times of their lives, we find it difficult to stay around. When my mother-in-law was dying, I thought that if I visited her every day, as I should have, as she would have visited me, my husband would think that was enough and wouldn't go visit his mother. What an excuse! One day I realized my error — call it the gift of the Spirit — and I snuck over to her hospice room and spent time with her. In our time alone, I was able to tell her what an awesome grandmother and mother-in-law she had been. She mouthed back very clearly and simply, "I love you." "I love you too." That was the greatest gift she could ever have given me.

Jesus wants us to stand by Him no matter where the path may lead, and He wants us to stand by one another. He knows that it will not be easy, but the payment is worth anything we may have to endure because of our commitment. The Kingdom . What more than to eat and to drink at His table? In the Kingdom.

November 13

"All of you will have your faith shaken, for it is written: / 'I will strike the shepherd, / and the sheep will be dispersed.'"

MARK 14:27

$\mathscr{E}$veryone wants to get in touch with the boss, the leader, the head because when it comes down to making a final decision, the buck stops with the boss. Sometimes I have to go out of town for the bookstore, and when I come back there are mounds of questions. It's not that someone else couldn't handle them, but they have their own jobs to do. The final decisions need to be made. I went to the Mid-South Leadership Conference, and when I came back there was much work to be done. A few things I had left with notes were still around with questions attached. Now we all know work was done, but the final decisions still had to be made. The bottom line answers still had to be given.

Jesus speaks to us about our faith. He knows that the minute we feel He is not in our midst, we panic. He is our shepherd, our leader, our boss. With Him, we are safe to walk in the light, to live in freedom, to be strong in our faith. Without Him, we live in fear, we shake. Jesus is our bottom line. He is the final answer. Do not let your faith be shaken. He remains.

November 14

"Simon, Simon, behold Satan has demanded to sift all of you like wheat, but I have prayed that your own faith may not fail; and once you have turned back, you must strengthen your brothers."

LUKE 22:31, 32

$\mathscr{I}$ sat in Sunday Mass awaiting my family's time for Communion. As we stood, I noticed two young boys, both dressed in seer-sucker pants and white pressed shirts, in the line. There must have been only a year difference in age, but the brother in front was fully turned toward his brother, walking backwards, showing him that he needed to cross his arms in front of his chest so the priest would know not to give him Communion. His arms were crossed so to try to get his brother's attention, he was kicking him. He wanted his brother to get the blessing, to strengthen his faith, and he was willing to bruise him, risk the anger of his dad, to accomplish his goal. Finally, right before the older brother's turn, the younger one snapped into holy mode, crossed his arms over his chest, and allowed his older brother to turn for his blessing.

Jesus is praying for us. He wants us to be strong in our faith. He wants us to strengthen one another. He knows that evil is alive and waiting, tempting us, so He prays and He will do anything to save us, spare us, to get us that single blessing so that we are strengthened to do the same for others. Turn around. Receive.

"Do not let your hearts be troubled. You have faith in God; have faith also in me."

JOHN 14:1

Little by little I am witnessing small businesses, and some larger ones, close. Businesses I have grown up supporting or known since childhood. I recently discovered that a prominent bookstore in our city is closing. Reality is frightening. There seems to be times in our lives, on this earth, when our world is more troubled than usual. When countries are at war, when leaders have tendencies to further their own lives instead of the lives of the people, we need the strength and the wisdom of Jesus Christ, of God, of the Holy Spirit, more than ever. We are troubled. We are in trouble. We trouble one another. In these times of crisis and uncertainty, when we are in pain and panicked by pain, we panic others, our neighbors.

Jesus speaks to us about our fear in difficult times. Do not be troubled. Have faith. He will bring us through these hard times. We experience losses all sorts of ways in our lives, but we must never lose our faith in the very One who will save us. Hold on to the One who will safeguard your heart. We are called to hold fast to our faith.

"In my Father's house there are many dwelling places. If there were not, would I have told you that I am going to prepare a place for you?"

JOHN 14:2

In our house we are fortunate to have space for each of us to be apart from one another or to be gathered all together in one room. A long 1960s ranch, the bedrooms are at one end with the playroom at the opposite end. As some children study, sleep, or need time alone, others can enjoy football games, visit with friends, or play games and not disturb the rest of the house. We also have a large yard where my husband finds peace, and a garage for him to hide when necessary. I often ride a mower to help out and to have time alone to think. The children have their own places in the yard or they can sit on the back patio. A large manhole cover sits between properties where a child is often sitting, stewing, mad as a hornet at something said or a game lost. The creek in the back yard is a peaceful place to get away. There are many places for this family of eight to enjoy together or to be alone.

Jesus gives us a glimpse of what is in store for us after this life. He knows each of us by name. He knows our needs and our wants and our expectations. He goes before us to make a place in His Father's house where we can dwell in our specifically prepared place for all eternity. Jesus is preparing for us to join Him. Prepare a place for Him. Prepare for others.

November 17

"I am the way and the truth and the life. No one comes to the Father except through me. If you know me, then you will also know my Father."
JOHN 14:6, 7

Everyone I meet who knows my dad says, "You're just like your father." They're right, and I'll take it. You see, my dad is a good man, but works hard not to let anyone know. The difference between us is that if I were half as good, I'd want everyone to know. He gives to area schools and churches, sponsors many underprivileged programs, and supports countless area projects, and no one would ever know. His name is nowhere to be seen. When recipients insist on recognizing his generosity, he often puts mom's business name, St. Mary's Bookstore. Being one who loves attention, I'm not really much like my dad, but I wish I were.

Jesus speaks to us about His Father. If we read and study and know about Jesus, we will also know His Father. Through Jesus we find our way. Through Jesus we find the truth. And through Jesus we have life, and we can have eternal life. Father and Son are One. May we love them. May we imitate them. May we long to be one with them. Take the time. Know Him.

"Have I been with you for so long a time and you still do not know me, Philip?"

JOHN 14:9

$\mathcal{A}$s we grow, we tend to change from being the goofy, crazy teens we once were to the "will you please take me seriously" adults we want to become. Often those I grew up with assume it is okay to tell their children, or worse my coworkers or neighbors, how mean I am or how crazy I can be. Do they not know me at all? I don't want my nieces and my nephews to fear me or to be afraid to come to my house. I adore them and would do anything for them. I do not want my peers to see me as the wild and crazy teen I once was. I certainly do not want my customers to question my sincerity. The past is the past. I'm a wife and a mom and a writer and a business owner. Do they still not know me?

Jesus shares with us the importance of really knowing the people He has put into our lives. He wants us to take time with them. Listen and grow. Allow others to mature with the friendship and the relationship. Know them where they have been, where they are going, and where they want to go. We are called to learn about others in our lives. Love them. Let them grow.

"And whatever you ask in my name, I will do, so that the Father may be glorified in the Son. If you ask anything of me in my name, I will do it."

JOHN 14:13, 14

$\mathcal{W}$hen my daughter was preparing for her First Communion, she shared that when she kneels during Benediction and begins to pray, "In the Name of the Father and of the Son and of the Holy Spirit," and crosses herself, she feels like she is knocking on Jesus' door. She's asking Him to open His door, and then she enters and sits in front of Him. He is behind a desk that is full of stacks of papers, questions, and prayer requests that people are constantly sending. Now I can't help but think that Jesus is pleased with this little girl knocking on His door as often as possible, and all of us as well. As I genuflect and cross myself entering the church pew, I think about Jesus letting me in. When I cross myself before the Rosary or confession, I think about Jesus opening that door. My daughter has given me a beautiful image of Jesus beckoning me to be with Him.

Jesus tells us that if we ask Him in His Name, He will give us what we ask. When He answers us, when He takes care of our needs, He glorifies His Father. The Father sent Him to save us, and He is here for us. Let us knock at His door. Ask in His Name. Jesus awaits.

November 20

"And I will ask the Father, and he will give you another Advocate to be with you always, the Spirit of truth, which the world cannot accept, because it neither sees nor knows it. But you know it, because it remains with you, and will be in you."

JOHN 14:16, 17

Even today, I love watching the movie *A Christmas Carol*. I love the visits from the Spirits of the Past, Present, and Future. Regardless of the version of the movie, Ebenezer Scrooge has a difficult time believing each of the Spirits until they prove themselves by dragging him all over his past, his present, and his future. Even then, when the Spirits leave, he tries to shake the image, "the dream," from his mind. But by morning the entire night's occurrence remains with him, and he is changed forever. Then, his change is for the rest of the world to accept. His transformation holds us in our seats and causes us to believe in the possibility of good in all people. The Spirits have brought truth, a truth that remains.

Jesus promises us a bonus, an added feature, someone extra to help us out. He gives us the Spirit of truth and, although He knows that not everyone will believe, He knows that we "get it." We remain with Him. We have dragged ourselves all around with Him for years and we know He remains in us. The Spirit of Truth remains.

November 21

"Peace I leave with you; my peace I give to you. Not as the world gives do I give it to you. Do not let your hearts be troubled or afraid."

JOHN 14:27

In the 1960s and 1970s, when I was growing up, the peace sign was huge. Of course, countries were at war, so there was always

197

talk of peace. There were pickets for peace and sit downs for peace and fighting for peace. World peace. Worldly peace. Hardly peaceful. Now it's the twenty-first century, and the peace sign is back. Jewelry and wall hangings and bumper stickers designed with the crow's feet inside a circle. Duplicate signs, the same fighting, similar wars, and talk of peace hover over our countries. Pickets and sit downs and rallies are different because of technology, but the messages are the same. Hardly peaceful.

Jesus speaks to us about true peace. Not the cycle of worldly peace, the physical type, but the peace of mind and peace of heart and peace of soul that only He can give. His peace is an inner calmness that if all would accept, the world would truly be peaceful, peace filled, at peace. Accept the gift He leaves us. Spread His peace.

November 22

"You are already pruned because of the word that I spoke to you."

JOHN 15:3

M y mother loved to have rose bushes in her yard. She had certain mixtures of plant food she'd concoct for them to grow beautiful blooms each year. She pruned them so they would produce more long stemmed, huge, beautiful flowers. She cut them back so they could produce fully. Her father, too, loved roses, and he passed on the passion and the mixture and the pruning. His heart was as big as the blooms of his flowers, and His love as bright as the red of the petals. Together they learned to prune so as to produce more fully the large red blossoms and the beautiful rose scent.

Jesus tells us that we have already been pruned. His words bring us life. His words allow us growth. His words fill us with all we need to color our world. He has cut us back, and we can now produce fully. May we learn to listen to His Word and remain full bodied, always producing large, fragrant results. Stay pruned. Produce.

November 23

"I am the vine, you are the branches. Whoever remains in me and I in him will bear much fruit, because without me you can do nothing."

JOHN 15:5

$\mathcal{L}$ ike most young kids, I had a best friend while growing up who stuck with me through thick and thin. We were better together. We could be completely ourselves around one another. What one couldn't do the other could. Together we were complete. We didn't have to try or to pretend or to fake it around one another. The way we were was good enough. We thought alike, could finish each other's sentences, and helped each other be the best or worst we could be. And then after grade school we were separated from one another and discovered we could make it on our own. We had probably strengthened one another along the way, but we were no longer completely dependent on one another.

Jesus wants us to realize that there are many people who come and go in our lives, but it is He alone who can sustain us. He alone is our true stability. He alone helps us to grow. He alone is all we really need to get us through this life. He gives us the people around us for support and for comfort, but when it comes down to it, we must learn to rely on Him. Him alone.

November 24

"If you keep my commandments, you will remain in my love, just as I have kept my Father's commandments and remain in his love. / I have told you this so that my joy might be in you and your joy might be complete."

JOHN 15:10, 11

$\mathcal{T}$ here is no greater joy for me than to witness my children loving one another. Before my youngest entered grade school, she would often wait behind our house until the three middle children could be seen walking through the neighbor's yard, and then she'd start running. The other children opened their arms wide and let her jump inside a hug. It was as if they hadn't seen one another in months. Oh the joy (mixed with a little drama)! They'd hand her a little something to carry and ask her about her day and she in turn would ask about their day.

Jesus tells us what we need to experience complete joy. He has joy because He has kept His Father's commands and He is willing to give that gift of joy to us. He wants us to imitate Him, to keep the commandments. He's standing in the back yard with His arms spread wide waiting to embrace us. We are asked to follow His commands. Remain in His love. Experience complete joy.

"I have called you friends, because I have told you everything I have heard from my Father. It was not you who chose me, but I who chose you and appointed you to go and bear fruit that will remain, so that whatever you ask the Father in my name he may give you."

JOHN 15:15, 16

Eenie meenie minee mo.... One potato, two potato, three potato, four.... When we were young, choosing a friend to do something or to be on our team was difficult amongst other friends. We played games to choose so we would not hurt anyone's feelings or make anyone angry. However, we hand-picked close friends to whom we told everything. Special friends were chosen for their faithfulness and trust. We chose carefully and only held on to the ones who were true to our trust. If we found a friend who could genuinely keep a secret, we formed a bond. True friendship is rare.

Jesus calls us to be His friend. He trusts us and appoints us to go and to make a difference in His name. We may ask, and He will give because of our close friendship and our faithfulness. He chooses us. We are hand-picked.

"If I had not come and spoken to them, they would have no sin; but as it is they have no excuse for their sin."

JOHN 15:22

I once had a young man stop by our bookstore and ask if he could repaint our faded signs. He needed the work, and our signs did need painting, so I walked around the building and showed him what I wanted. All of our signs were blue except for the "more" in "more than a bookstore" so I wanted to be clear as to our expectations. Well, he had plenty of red paint so he decided that the side sign would stand out more if it were all red. As you can imagine, businesses do not like to be in the red. When I told him he had to repaint it, he gave plenty of excuses why his idea was better. "But I told you blue so please change it." No excuse.

Jesus tells us that we have no excuse to sin. We have the opportunity to read His words and obey His commandments. He is truth. He has come, and He walks among us. He speaks. We listen to His teachings. We are asked to learn His ways and remain free from sin. Ignorance is not bliss. If we follow Him and His teachings, we will find true happiness. No excuse.

November 27

"But I tell you the truth, it is better for you that I go. For if I do not go, the Advocate will not come to you. But if I go, I will send him to you."

JOHN 16:7

Many parents choose to home school their children, and I am in constant awe of their abilities to master the roles of wife, mother, and teacher. I personally could never handle such a challenge. In my life, some of my greatest support comes from the wonderful teachers, my advocates, who are placed in the lives of my children. These teachers do not just teach, but they work on our behalf to help our children to a better way through life. We are fortunate.

Jesus speaks to us about sending the Advocate. He leaves us in the hands of the One who will support us in this life. He leaves us with the One who can save us and who can help us to overcome ourselves. Jesus does not leave us alone, but leaves us in the hands of the One who can work on our behalf and help us to a better way through life. We are called to follow the One Jesus has sent. Allow the Advocate to come.

November 28

"Amen, amen, I say to you, you will weep and mourn, while the world rejoices; you will grieve, but your grief will become joy."

JOHN 16:20

I remember thinking after my nephew died, "How can these people go around doing regular day to day activities and talking and laughing when my family is mourning such a great loss?" When my friend died suddenly I thought, "How can these people be playing golf when I just lost my golf partner?" When my brother died, I dared anyone to ask why I was not at work. How could they not know? There is definitely something to be said about a period of mourning, a time to be left alone. But truth is, the world goes on and so must we.

Jesus tells us that we will have to endure a certain amount of sadness and grief while on this earth. He knows the ways of this world. He knows what it's like to experience a loss. But He also knows what awaits us in our reward of Heaven. He tells us to endure the pain because it will not be forever. Grief will become joy.

November 29

"When a woman is in labor, she is in anguish because her hour has arrived; but when she has given birth to a child, she no longer remembers the pain because of her joy that a child has been born into the world."
JOHN 16:21

I can never forget the birth of each of my children. The surprise of discovering she's a girl or he's a boy. I remember the day of changing from operating room to delivery room, the opportunity for my mother to watch the birth, and how much more relaxed my husband was from the first birth to the last. I know that each of the labor and deliveries were different; each as unique as the child. I have seen no miracle greater than the birth of a child. Somehow I was able to go through the labor time and time again, not remembering the pain but rather the moment that precious child was placed in my arms.

Jesus shares with us the joy of bringing children into the world. He knows the pain involved in laboring for something so precious. Often, the very thing that brings us the most pain while experiencing or laboring over it, results in the greatest joy in our lives. Joy replaces pain.

November 30

"I have told you this in figures of speech. The hour is coming when I will no longer speak to you in figures but I will tell you clearly about the Father."
JOHN 16:25

*D*on't disturb the apple cart." I was fortunate one summer to talk my brother and his wife into letting me take their children for several days while they worked to sell his furniture in a temporary booth at the Atlanta Merchandise Mart. To me, the more children occupying one another the better as far as I was concerned. Everyone in the family offered all sorts of help, and my standard response was always, "As long as it does not disturb the apple cart." The last thing I needed during those days was to have the apples all over creation instead of simply in the same cart, stacked tightly, supporting one another.

Jesus speaks to us in ways that we can handle at the time and understand as it pertains to a situation. He tells us that all will eventually be clear to us. His words will make sense, His stories will be understood, and those who stick with Him will be enlightened. Even when His words are difficult to follow in our world today, we are called to stay close to Him so all will be seen. Seen clearly.

December 1

"I have told you this so that you might have peace in me. In the world you will have trouble, but take courage, I have conquered the world."

JOHN 16:33

Working in a small retail business, along with the joys, we definitely have our troubles. The Internet seems to be taking a toll on sales. Electronic readers are affecting the demand for books. The economy weighs on people's ability to give to the Church, which directly affects our Church goods business. Mega warehouse companies can undersell us at every turn. But not one of these avenues can beat us in service, in atmosphere or in hands-on, feel-good sincerity. In one way or another, there is always competition, setbacks, and challenges. There is always a way to reorganize, to cut back, and to conquer. There will always be troubles because it is the way of the world, but through those times we must take courage and find a better way. For it is not for this world that we persist.

Jesus calls us to a realization. There will be troubles in this world. They will be temporary. We must drag ourselves through the muck and stay focused on a better way. Jesus has already won the fight and prepared a place for us. Each day we must have courage. Think positive. Jesus has conquered the world. Each day we must choose to change our attitude. Enjoy peace in Him.

"Now this is eternal life, that they should know you, the only true God, and the one whom you sent, Jesus Christ."

JOHN 17:3

*B*efore we promise to "love and honor all the days of our lives," we had better make sure we truly know the person we have chosen. To know someone, really know them, we have to spend time with them and talk to and listen to and hear them. I love the idea that in our daughters' high school, the girls are asked to put together a book about their future marriage. They are asked to make lists of possible dates they can go on to help them know their future spouse better. They are taught to pray for their future spouse. It's not about having to get married or pushing marriage, but it's about preparing for a possible vocation. Honestly, I know it took my husband and me quite a few years of trial and error to get to know each other, and we still work at it every day, as we should.

Jesus gives us a glimpse into eternal life. We must know the Father and His Son, and He means know them. We would have to visit them often and spend time with them. We should feel comfortable as soon as our feet cross the threshold of their home. Maybe we need to prepare for our time together and think of ways to renew and refresh the relationship. We are challenged to talk and to listen and to hear and to know the "only true God" and "Jesus Christ." Now that is eternal life!

"I pray for them. I do not pray for the world but for the ones you have given me, because they are yours, and everything of mine is yours and everything of yours is mine, and I have been glorified in them."

JOHN17:9, 10

*M*any times I have heard my mom say, "You know, all we can do is pray for them." As usual, she's right. People need prayers, and prayers work. I have been fortunate to join with hundreds of others in praying for specific people. We print holy cards and pass them out by the hundreds for all to join us in prayer for healing. Sometimes our prayers are answered with physical healing, and sometimes they are answered with healing that is more difficult to understand. But prayers are answered. I have watched a young girl fight a battle for years only to die after multiple operations and visits to the hospital. And yet, I watched the world around her, those she came in contact with, nurses, doctors, friends, and family, change. Many of the people she touched changed because of her incredible faith and trust in God. She prayed with us, she shared stories, and she loved the short, intense life she was given.

Jesus prays for us. What more could we possibly need than His prayers to His Father for us? He knows what this world has to offer, and He knows the difficulties we will have to face each day. He prays for us, specifically, and He wants us to pray for one another. Not for the world, but for the people. Pray.

December 4

"Consecrate them in the truth. Your word is truth. As you sent me into the world, so I sent them into the world."

JOHN 17:17, 18

When I was in grade school, my first principal was a very good friend of my mother. Sr. Jane Dominic made life in the early grades very good for me. She often called me to the office, getting me out of class to meet someone who had come by her office who knew my mother or simply to share some ice cream. I was sent to run errands quite frequently. Sr. Jane Dominic had a way of making me and many of the other students feel special. She had specific duties she saved for certain students.

We are consecrated in truth. We are dedicated to a specific service. We are chosen, and we are sent out in the world just as Jesus was sent to the world. We must find that purpose. The truth is in His word. We must read, and we must learn, and we must take what He gives out to the world. Jesus gives us purpose. We are called to follow the word and continue the lesson.

December 5

"And I have given them the glory you gave me, so that they may be one, as we are one, I in them and you in me, that they may be brought to

perfection as one, that the world may know that you sent me, and that you loved them even as you loved me."

JOHN 17:22, 23

There are certain aspects of my life that work perfectly when everyone around me works together as one. I'm sure that's true for most of us. At one point in our married lives, Allen and I had children in four schools. Four schools meant four schedules, and our family working as one meant success. The high school girl was first up and first out, followed by the son in kindergarten at a different school, then the three in grade school, and finally my daughter in day care. If one section of our routine was held up in any way, the next sections were late for school. We are best when we work as one.

Jesus wants us to work as one with Him so that we may one day be brought to perfection in His love. We have to pay attention. We have to stay close to Him. We have to understand that this world will eat us up if we allow. Our human selves are weak, but He has given us His Spirit who will take over any time we call upon Him. We are not to live in regret. We are called to plan and to pray so that all aspects of our lives work together to bring us to Him. In glory.

December 6

"Father, they are your gift to me. I wish that where I am they also may be with me, that they may see my glory that you gave me, because you loved me before the foundation of the world."

JOHN 17:24

I often travel alone for business. Friends say, "Oh awesome. You get to be all by yourself in a hotel without any children. Lucky you." And at the time, I agree. "Yes, lucky me." But once I get to the place, it never fails that I wish my children and my husband were with me. There's usually a nice pool and a nice workout area and fun shopping close by and a room way too big for one person. I always wish my children could see the big city at night or the small town with its unique shops and eating places. I wish my husband could eat a nice dinner at the places I go with the people I meet. My husband and children are my gift, and I wish they were with me.

Jesus speaks of us as being a gift to Him. We are given as gifts, and we are loved, and He wants us to be with Him. He has all these awesome things to show us. We are given to Him. We are loved. We are called to remain in that love. He wishes us to be with Him. Stay close to Him.

December 7

"My Father, if it is possible, let this cup pass from me; yet, not as I will, but as you will."

MATTHEW 26:39

From what I could understand, the man was a German soldier. He was ushering families to the trains that would eventually take them to the prison camps. The woman was in the line to board the train when the German soldier pulled her aside. She had a full head of beautiful blond hair and a sweet smile that would melt a young man's heart. Thankfully, the German soldier noticed her. The in-between of the story was completely left out, but the outcome was a wedding and a forever marriage filled with love and honor. Together they would move to America and raise a family in the faith clinging to the same God that allowed her cup to pass. God's will be done.

Jesus speaks to His Father today and teaches us again about prayer. He asks His Father if He could possibly keep Him from His impeding suffering, but He knows that the Father can only do what is best for the whole world. He prays understanding that His will be done. As we pray may we too understand that in asking we must not ask what we will for ourselves, but what God wills for us. He knows what's ahead. He knows what's best. God's will be done.

December 8

"Watch and pray that you may not undergo the test. The spirit is willing, but the flesh is weak."

MATTHEW 26:41

I have played out hundreds of scenarios in my life where I've not done things I've wanted to do. My mind says "go" but my body says "no" types of things. Many scenes include the homeless or the poor or a sudden misfortune when I have held back out of sheer fear. Other scenes include life choices when I've just not moved forward out of lack of preparation or due to plain laziness. Shoulda, coulda, woulda … I call these times in my life. Shoulda gone to a small college, coulda played basketball, woulda loved it. Shoulda thought more about my future, coulda taken business classes, woulda been a better store manager. I'm not stuck in regrets; I'm just sharing that I should have followed more with my heart and my soul, then my body.

Jesus tells us that our bodies are our weak links. Inside each of us there is a spirit that can take care of everything we have set in front of us, but our human selves hold us back. We must keep watch. We must pray every day, all day. We are weak, but He is willing to take care of us. We are called to go to Him and remain with Him always. Follow the Spirit.

December 9

"Sit here while I pray."

MARK 14:32

I could never forget when my mom and two daughters, Beth and Sarah, and I, while traveling in Spain, took the train, landed in Ávila, took a taxi to the center of town, and then entered the small church in the square. My mom noticed they were about to start Mass and asked if we would mind waiting as she attended. No problem. To this day, I cannot for the life of me think why we did not go in to Mass too. She asked us to wait and we did. But why on earth we did not join her I cannot remember. For some reason the short separation happened, and it was something necessary for the moment.

Jesus asks us just to sit. Sit. He'll do the work. He'll take care of us. He is in prayer. Maybe we are to pray or to listen or just to wait, but we are called to sit in His midst. Have patience. Relax. Wait.

December 10

"I told you that I AM. So if you are looking for me, let these men go."

JOHN 18:8

*W*ere you looking for me?" I walked down front to take care of William, my regular street person. William has a home and a family and he has something wrong with him that obviously happened years ago. God bless him. He wanders up and down the main street of Nashville killing time. The people at our bookstore try to save me the time of talking with him day after day, but hey, I'm here. Let's hear it all again. Some days, by the time I get down front he's busy hugging and shaking hands with customers and asking questions about the availability of jobs or cars or motorcycles. Once he gets going, he cannot control himself. "Come on, William. I'm here now. Let these people go back to what they were doing."

Jesus is here. Now. We can let go of all that simply occupies our time and our energy and direct all our needs toward Him. He is all we have been looking for even when we do not realize that He is the answer. He has told us many times, and yet He tells us over again. Let all else go. Release the many things of this world that hold us back and let Him approach. He is here.

December 11

"I have spoken publicly to the world. I have always taught in a synagogue or in the temple area where all the Jews gather, and in secret I have said nothing."

JOHN 18:20

I told everyone the same thing. When I coached volleyball, invariably I'd get a girl who came late for an unusual practice time, and she'd say, "You never told us we had to come. I thought it was a choice. Sorry I'm late, but I decided last minute...." "Start running." "But coach." "Run." Every other girl heard the same message and everyone else was on time and ready to get started. This was no secret meeting. This was no surprise. She was getting no sympathy or preferential treatment. She had to suffer the consequence no matter how small the offense. She disturbed the already begun practice.

Jesus tells us that what He has said, He has given openly and freely, and it is available to all people. Through Scripture, through the teachings of the Church, His words are for everyone. Everyone is hearing the same message so we can all be on the same page. There should be no disturbances. His words will save us. No secrets. All we have to do is show up. We are called to read. And to listen.

"Why ask me? Ask those who heard me what I said to them. They know what I said."

JOHN 18:21

I don't know. But I'll find out." That is the typical answer from me as I work in our bookstore. Customers rely on us to know about the faith, about prayer, about spirituality, about books, and about product. And we should know, to a point. We have everything known to man about the Catholic Faith at our fingertip. Most of our products come with information about how they were made or the artist who designed it. Reading, listening, researching, and knowing all seems to pay off for our customers. If we don't know the answer, we can usually find it.

Jesus tells us that there are plenty of people around us who are listening to Him. There are many who are passing on His teachings in books and through speaking engagements and by example. We are to know what is available to us. We are to go to the retreats and the lectures and read the books and listen at Mass, and we are to hear what Jesus is saying so we can know Him. Why ask, when we can get the Answer for ourselves? We are called to participate in His life with the many others who hear. Know what is said.

"If I tell you, you will not believe, and if I question, you will not respond."

LUKE 22:67, 68

My youngest brother has an incredible way of telling the most far-fetched stories. First, he always has to stand because his animated delivery brings forth more laughter. Then, he proceeds to "hip-up" his pants with his elbows and settle in. He tells this unbelievable story of freeing a peanut butter jar from the nose of a raccoon. A thirty to forty-five minute ordeal only to end with the raccoon being freed, taking a deep gulping breathe of air, and diving back into the jar full throttle. His crazy stories make me wonder if he just happens upon the oddest situations or if he can just embellish to please a crowd like no other. The stories are hard to believe, and if we question, he doesn't respond to the question but uses it to further the impossibility of the situation.

Jesus calls us to believe in Him. He knows the reality of some-one coming to die for us, to give up His life to save us, and to love us unconditionally is unthinkable. He knows there is nothing we can say in response to His love for us. And it's all okay. We need not say anything. All He asks is that we listen and learn and love one another. Just love one another.

"Do you say this on your own or have others told you about me?"

JOHN 18:34

*P*redetermined opinion. I have consciously been thinking how gossip predetermines people's opinions of others. My biggest sin is talking about others. Most of the time I'm joking around about someone, laughing about an occurrence or what someone else has said. I went to confession about gossiping, and a priest challenged me to think about telling the person that I was laughing about something they said or did. Suddenly all the fun and laughter is gone, and I have to think about whether or not the person I'm gossiping about would be laughing with us or would feel hurt or angry. Could I actually be hurting their reputation? The people I talk to may never in this lifetime meet those I talk about, but if they did, would they form their own opinion, or would what I have done or said be stuck in their minds?

Jesus questions how we form opinions about one another. Do we listen to what others say and judge, or do we take the time to really know someone and let all gossip fall by the wayside? Even more, do we add fuel to the fire? Do we start rumors? What we say and who we say it to and what we repeat matters. Jesus wants us to take the time to know one another. And to know Him.

"Everyone who belongs to the truth listens to my voice."

JOHN 18:37

I never realized what people heard when they listened to my voice until I heard myself on tape. Horror stories! When my parents had their fiftieth wedding anniversary, I wrote a song and had my brothers who live in North Carolina record it. To give them the tune, I sang a few lines on my brother's answering machine. Those two said they laughed until they couldn't breathe. I tried to sing in this high voice instead of my regular voice. They loved the lyrics but could not believe anyone could sing so ridiculously. It was unnatural. They played it over and over in disbelief.

Jesus speaks of His voice. We know to listen to that voice, to belong to the truth, we must be silent. We must stop trying to speak or sing in different ways just to be heard. Be natural. He wants us to be ourselves. If we want the truth, if we want to belong to the truth, we must listen over and over. Everyone wants to belong.

December 16

"Father, forgive them, they know not what they do."

LUKE 23:34

In our family, joking around can sometimes cause pain. One of my mom's favorite sayings is, "It's all fun and games until someone loses an eye." She has pointed more wooden spoons in our direction with warnings attached than I can count on fingers and toes. Seems she's always working in the kitchen when the poking and prodding begins. We do not set out to hurt anyone, but words and actions can get out of hand. When we were kids, we all knew not to tease Phillip about too much because he would settle things right in the middle of the living room floor. The wrestling match usually ended in a lamp broken or a bloody nose and a bunch of apologies. Oh there are always many apologies.

Jesus prays to His Father to forgive the people who have done Him wrong. He knows that many times people do and say things out of ignorance and, despite all the warnings, never quite understand the consequences. We are called to forgive all that is said about us and all that is done to us. We are to believe that others do not realize the harm they can cause, and we are to realize how our words and our actions can affect others. Forgive and be forgiven.

December 17

"Woman, behold, your son."

JOHN 19:26

When I was presented with my first child, there was an instinct in me that immediately turned to mother. I was just a girl like any other turned suddenly into a mother, a woman, the one a child would turn to in need, the one a child would turn to in hunger, the one who would satisfy, who would nourish, and who would be depended on. Each time that child lay in my arms, I knew that she was mine and I was hers, completely.

Jesus gives us His Mother as woman, as mother. We are her sons and daughters. She is our mother. We can call upon her to intercede for us. Just as a child goes to his mother and asks her to ask dad for something, so too we can go to Mary, our Mother. We are hers. We are His, completely.

"Amen, I say to you, today you will be with me in Paradise."

LUKE 23:43

My parents have a home in Naples, Florida, that I call Paradise. There are no needs there, no clocks to live by, and no decisions to make except where to eat. My brother Pat calls it Fantasy Island. How true. In their home, the coffee in the morning is freshly brewed one cup at a time. The balconies overlook the Gulf, and looking out the windows we can see a golf course or the beach or tennis courts or a pool. After we walk through the parking lot, a shuttle drives us through a nature preserve where we watch for families of ducks and turtles or catch a glimpse of the alligators. New life is constant. The boardwalk crosses over an inlet where people rent canoes and enjoy the area between land and beach. As we enter the area before the beach there are restaurants. Bright blue lounge chairs, cabanas, and beach umbrellas wait as we enter the beach. The Gulf is clear and beautiful, and the sand is covered with shells. An occasional school of dolphins passes. There is excitement, there is beauty, and there is peace. We call it Paradise.

Jesus calls us to be with Him in Paradise. He calls us to a place where there will be no worries, no decisions, and no time constraints. He reaches out to us, and all we have to do is follow Him. We are called to new life. We are called to cross over and to accept His invitation. He wants us with Him. May we, some day, join Him. In Paradise.

"I thirst."

JOHN 19:28

When we do not drink the proper amount of fluids, our bodies give us a signal. We may have leg cramps or our skin is extremely dry or we are just point blank thirsty. No matter what the symptoms, we know we are lacking fluid, and we know what to do to get our bodies back on track. When I started having babies, I realized that my hair was brittle, my skin was dry, and I had extreme leg cramps almost daily. Those little ones were sucking the life out of me, and I had to replenish fluids double-time. Our bodies need water.

Jesus is thirsty. He is human. He is in need. As Christmas morning nears, may we consider what we can do to satisfy Jesus' thirst. He desires our time and our attention both for Himself and for each other. We must replenish ourselves so that we can in turn have enough to satisfy our God and our fellow man. Jesus thirsts. Fill His cup, and in so doing, fulfill the needs of others. Replenish. Satisfy.

"Oh, how foolish you are! How slow of heart to believe all that the prophets spoke!"

LUKE 24:25

Many times in my life I have heard what I believe is the same message over and over, and each time that is exactly how I receive it, as if I have heard it all before and "Here we go again." As I have read and listened to certain authors and speakers, I have learned that many are giving the same message, but I am hearing it now at a different time in my faith journey. I can even hear myself say, "I've heard this but never quite understood it the way it has been explained today." Sort of like when our parents have been telling us the same thing for years, but when we hear it from someone else it is a great revelation. My parents must think all the time, "It's been a slow process, but she seems to be getting there."

Jesus gets in our face about our slow belief. He's done it all for us. He has become man. He has sent prophets to teach us the truth. He sends many men and women daily who have had similar experiences and have come to believe and to draw us closer to Him. We are called to step up our pace. We are challenged to move along in our faith. He knows we are in a different place in our journey, but He sends the challenge. Attend more. Read more. Hear more. Pay attention. Believe.

December 21

"Peace be with you. As the Father has sent me, so I send you."

JOHN 20:21

The month of December is often a hectic month in my family. Running a retail business with our main focus on Jesus, and preparing six children plus adults for the birth of Christ, along with school projects, exams, and basketball keeps us moving in more than one direction. We are not unlike many families today. During what should be the most peaceful time of year, we find ourselves busy. We search for what brings peace.

Jesus sends us out. He does not want us to be complacent, to sit in our rooms and our homes and our jobs and be satisfied. He wants us to go out, and he wants us to be at peace with our going and our coming. We are called in this often-hectic world to find peace and to take it to others. Especially now.

December 22

"Receive the holy Spirit."

JOHN 20:22

I love to receive mail, especially personal mail that comes when I least expect it. I receive email all day long, everyday, and that is nice, but I mean I love to receive the old fashion handwritten snail mail. I open my mailbox in the afternoons and sort through the stack quickly to see if there is anything for me. If there happens to be something other than a bill, I savor the moment. I check the postmark and look for a return address, and upon finding one, pause and wonder what on earth this person could be sending me. My children each say, "Just open it already," but I like the whole process. I like to make the joy of receiving last just a moment longer. Even after I open and read personal mail, I oftentimes hold onto it to read again later. I may put it in my desk drawer or put it amongst a project I'm working on. I may read it again later in the day or later in the year. I love handwritten, personal mail.

Jesus gives us a huge gift. He wants us to receive the Holy Spirit, who will be with us to guide us through our entire lives. We must hold onto this moment, this gift. He must take time day after day to call upon the Holy Spirit for guidance and confirmation. He is with us now. The third person of the Trinity remains. We savor the moment. We hold the gift. We are enlightened.

December 23

"Why are you troubled? And why do questions arise in your hearts?"

LUKE 24:38

Two days before Christmas, and I can't help but be anxious. Have I gotten everything done? Is my family really on track for the birth of Jesus, or are they all about receiving presents for themselves? Will others like what I bought them? Do I even know the person I bought a gift for? Did I take time to try to get them something with meaning to their lives or did I just get them a gift? I truthfully want others to like what I give them. Like one who wants to be a millionaire, I may poll my family, reduce my choices, and/or phone a friend. I have a strange desire to satisfy. Even after given options, I am anxious to see their faces when they open the gift. Did I get the right information from their spouse? Did I get the proper brand? Were they surprised? Excited?

Jesus asks us today about our concerns. He is worried about us. He cares that we are worked up about so many trivial things in this world. He wonders why we have so many doubts and fears when He is right here with us. We are called to trust and to let go of all our worries and our concerns. He is here for us. All is well.

December 24

"Put your finger here and see my hands, and bring your hand and put it into my side, and do not be unbelieving, but believe."

JOHN 20:27

Christmas is a time of believing. Children believe they will get everything they ever wanted. Parents believe they can give presents that will make everyone happy. There is a spirit of giving and receiving that is magical, worth believing in. Christians believe that long ago a small child was born who will save the world. We believe the shepherds and the kings were led to a small stable in Bethlehem to give homage and gifts to a newborn king. We have not seen, but we believe. We tried as children to stay up all night to see Santa, but we knew that if we did not sleep Santa would not show up. The true miracle of Christmas is in the magic, the mystery, and the love.

On this day before His birth, we are told to believe. He was born a man, He came to save the world, and we are to believe and to welcome Him into our hearts and our homes as we celebrate the day of His birth. Believe in Him, although we cannot touch or see. Believe in the magic. Believe in the mystery.

December 25

"Blessed are those who have not seen and have believed."

JOHN 20:29

Every family celebrates Christmas day with different traditions. Some open a gift after midnight Mass and then finish the next morning. Some go to Mass first on Christmas morning, then open and exchange presents afterwards. Some attend a children's Mass the night before, then have the entire morning to watch as children open gifts and shriek with delight. But the fact is that most of the families I know include Mass or Church in their Christmas tradition even if they do not attend during any other time of year. The fact is that deep down, in our hearts, we all truly believe even though we were not there to see. And today we are blessed because of our belief.

We celebrate the birth of Jesus Christ. He was born into this world and all we are asked to do today is to believe and be blessed because of that belief. Believe in the miracle. We are blessed.

"Cast the net over the right side of the boat and you will find something."

JOHN 21:6

owadays, most items come with very little instruction, maybe pictures in suggested sequence or words in a foreign language. I have put together displays for our bookstore and furniture for our house and doll houses and bicycles. But I have to admit, there is one toy that never turns out quite right unless each and every direction is followed in order to the letter. That is Legos. I have helped my son put together numerous complicated Lego toys piece-by-piece, instruction-by-instruction. I have to say though, once the project falls apart, he discovers entire new worlds with the pieces. He turns the one big thing into many little cool items entirely with his imagination.

Jesus wants us to follow His instructions and change things around a little. The discoveries when we do follow Him are amazing. He always has more for us than we ever expect. We are to do as He asks, to listen to his directions, and to discover a whole new life with Him. Instruction by instruction He can turn one big thing into so much more. Discover something new.

"Feed my lambs."

JOHN 21:15

hen I first started working at St. Mary's Bookstore, I worked with two elderly women who remained with the store after my mom had purchased it from the Diocese. Both women were a big help, teaching me the ins and outs of the business. Both women helped by teaching me to get over myself and focus on the work in our midst. Countless days I watched "Red" care for the community. Not only did she serve those who came to shop, but she served all who came to chat and all who came to be fed in other ways. "Red" never had much, never made much, never needed much, but what she had, she shared. One woman in particular pushed a grocery cart filled with her life. She brought Red coupons every week, coupons she never used, in exchange for money. She treated the woman with dignity, allowed her to take the time to talk about the coupons and her needs, and then handed her some money. Even when we changed locations, Red told some of her "friends" where we could be found.

Jesus tells us to feed His lambs. He desires us to take care of those smaller than us in this world. He desires for us to take care of one another, to serve one another, not just physically, but to take time to feed the body and the soul. People need to be loved and to maintain their dignity through all the rough times in life. Feed His people.

December 28

"Amen, amen, I say to you, when you were younger, you used to dress yourself and go where you wanted; but when you grow old, you will stretch out your hands, and someone else will dress you and lead you where you do not want to go."

JOHN 21:18

I watched my grandmother closely in her elderly years. She was an amazing woman; a survivor of wars, depression, and change, and a woman of faith, virtue, and dignity. I watched as she allowed herself to be taken care of after my grandfather's death. I watched as she allowed herself to follow other's schedules for her. She did not always want to eat at certain times or wake at certain times, but she followed their plans. In humility she allowed her caretakers to care for her how they saw fit. She was a strong woman who made those who cared for her enjoy the time. She lived to be 100 and was a delight to all around her.

Jesus speaks to us about life and death. He speaks to us about freedom in our youth. He speaks to us about constraints as we grow old. In the Bible context, He speaks of His impending death on the cross, but for us today there is more in His words. How we live, how we treat others, how we allow others to be a part of our lives, how we act and react are all a part of our days, our moments in our journey back to Him. We must use time wisely. Allow others to feel good about themselves. Love all.

"What if I want him to remain until I come? What concern is it of yours? You follow me."

JOHN 21:22

When you have several children, it never fails that one or two always feel like they are doing more work than the others. "Life's not fair." A simple task like bringing in the groceries and putting them away can bring out the worst in children around our house. Someone's always late coming to help and then argues about putting things away. I generally could care less who does what as long as it all gets done, but the children seem to care about everything from closing the back of the van to putting the last can of corn in the Lazy Susan. As I drive up the driveway, they are in each other's business. I call the boys to unload the car and get the girls to follow me to the kitchen, but someone always sways off the path. "We'd get finished faster if you just worked and didn't argue." "Who cares?" "Stop worrying about her."

Jesus calls us to mind our own business. It is no concern of ours to worry about what He does for others. It is not our job to compare. We are simply to follow. Today and every day, follow.

"And behold, I am with you always, until the end of the age."

MATTHEW 28:20

I have certain people in my life I can always count on regardless the hour of the day or the day of the week. I have certain ones who have been around since my childhood, and I count myself very fortunate that they have remained in my life. No matter my mishaps or misgivings, they remain. No matter my mood or my needs, they remain. No matter my joys or my sorrows, they have been here through the thick of it all and they will be here until the end of my time. They have shown me unconditional love all the days of my life.

Jesus tells us that He will be with us forever. What better news could we possibly hear? It will not matter our mood or our circumstance or our faults or our needs. Jesus is with us always. Behold, until the end.

"Go into the whole world and proclaim the gospel to every creature."

MARK 16:15

After attending a three-day retreat, I was completely pumped up, filled with the Holy Spirit and ready to spread the Good News to everyone. The entire weekend I heard that this "fourth day" would be an emotional high, a wonderful day. I rose early and read the day's Scripture and wrote in my journal. After taking the children to school, I went to Mass. I went home and called my sister and shared my weekend experience. I went to school and joined my children for lunch. I took time with my family and my friends and shared my faith. I phoned a friend who made the retreat with me and explained my day and shared my complete exhaustion. She said, "Did you read the booklet we were given about our fourth day?" "Not yet, I haven't had time." "The fourth day is the rest of our lives." I sank back in my chair. How could I keep this pace my entire life?

One full year of the words of Jesus, and we are challenged to go out and tell the world all we have heard. What an incredible journey! What a wonderful challenge. This is our fourth day. On this last day of the year may we challenge ourselves to continue His journey, His life, and His teachings. May we be His voice in this world and proclaim His Gospel message. Speak His words. Deliver His message. Every day.